Catholic Social Teaching and Distributism

Toward a New Economy

Michael Hickey

Hamilton Books

Lanham • Boulder • New York • Toronto • Plymouth, UK

4501 Forbes Boulevard, Suite 200, Lanham, Maryland 20706
Hamilton Books Acquisitions Department (301) 459-3366

Unit A, Whitacre Mews, 26-34 Stannary Street,
London SE11 4AB, United Kingdom

Printed in the United States of America
British Library Cataloguing in Publication Information Available

Library of Congress Control Number: 2017953695
ISBN: 978-0-7618-7004-3 (pbk : alk. paper)—ISBN: 978-0-7618-7005-0 (electronic)

∞™ The paper used in this publication meets the minimum requirements of American National Standard for Information Sciences Permanence of Paper for Printed Library Materials, ANSI/NISO Z39.48-1992.

"Who, then, is the faithful and prudent servant,
to whom the master has put in charge of his household
to distribute to them their food at the proper time (Mt 24:45)?"

Contents

The Cover

The use of the phrase “In God We Trust” on U.S. currency first appeared in 1864. Salmon P. Chase, Treasury Secretary, under Abraham Lincoln wanted to give some recognition to God in a national motto. The phrase eventually found its way onto all U.S. currency around the same time that “under God” was added to the Pledge of Allegiance and as part of the cultural war against atheistic communism. A 1955 vote of the U.S. Congress elected to officially place the motto on all U.S. money.

The phrase, however, is far more generic and less specific than the imagery of the pyramid (representing the Trinity) and the “Eye of Providence” on the back of the one-dollar bill. The all-seeing eye of God was to represent the many ways in which Providence was to favor the American cause. The Eye of Providence, when placed together with the eagle holding 13 arrows (representing the 13 original states), then constitutes the Great Seal of the United States which was approved by congress in 1782.

The word, “Providence,” means “making provision for the future,” and comes from the Latin, *pro-videre* which means “to see ahead.” It refers to Divine foresight in shaping history and every human being in history. Essentially, it corresponds to God’s grace-filled guidance and loving care for us as God sees all there is that constitutes history past, present, and future.

Providence occurs at the intersection of God’s sovereignty and our human free will. Here, you cannot emphasize the power of God so strongly that it ends up negating our free will, nor can you emphasize our human freedom so much that God ends up not being omniscient and is limited. You cannot take history out of God’s hands or ours. But one of the big differences, however, is that God “sees ahead.” We don’t have that luxury and the only way we can possibly “see ahead,” like the Eye of Providence, is to unconsciously have the same vision God has. This we can never be sure of.

In this book, I assume that because God's eye sees everything, the Divine is very much interested in the cause of distributive justice both ethically and economically. I make this assumption based on the many times that God has said so, through the Bible and the prophets, through many of God's holy people throughout history, and particularly through every modern Papal Social Encyclical of the Catholic Church since 1891. These all constitute what is called today, "Catholic Social Teaching." There is not one Social Letter authored by any of the Holy Fathers since that time over one hundred years ago, that doesn't refer to the cause of distributive justice in the world. The modern Popes speak strongly in favor of it in each of these Social Letters and speak out strongly against the many structures and institutions that perpetuate distributive injustices and are present in the current society and economy.

So, if we believe that the all-seeing God, through the Eye of Providence has this vision of distributive justice, then we should probably line up with it is as best we can even though we'll never be certain we see it clearly, due to what the Gospels refer to as "The plank in our eye (MT. 7: 3-5)."

Section One:
Themes of Catholic Social Teaching

Chapter One

Beginnings and History

Catholic Social Teaching, (hereafter CST), is a source of Catholic doctrine that has historically been developed through the Tradition of the Catholic Church. Many Catholics don't realize that it's an essential part of our faith. For the most part, it is not taught in our Catholic schools, education programs, seminaries, colleges, and universities. However, every Catholic should understand how this teaching, rooted in the Bible and our Tradition, particularly the modern Papal Social Letters, calls us to choose life. It also insists that we honor human dignity, love God and our neighbor, and serve the least among us as we hunger for social justice and righteousness.

CST is complex because it is linked with many social questions which are constantly changing and because our understanding of the role of God in history is always deepening. The goal of this book will be to suggest that Catholic education and catechetical programs recognize its value and begin to incorporate it into the mainstream of church adult teaching and formation as it is essential to our identity as Catholics and central to the evangelizing mission of our church.

CST is certainly a part of Catholic Theology and belongs principally to the field of Moral Theology. This theology attempts to pull together many seemingly diverse issues pertaining to Sacred Scripture and Tradition; economics, poverty and wealth, theology and philosophy, politics and sociology, most particularly as they pertain to matters of social and distributive justice. The Church's social teaching is a rich treasure of Catholic thought concerning the building of a just society. The entire body of teaching implies putting persons before money, systems, structures, institutions, corporations, governments, or any other thing. To attempt to sum up the essence of CST with one simple statement: it calls for putting "people before things."

The history of CST is rooted in thousands of years of Judeo-Christian Tradition, but its history as a body of particular Catholic doctrine really is said to have had its beginning in 1891 with the writing of a Papal Encyclical (Letter) written by Pope Leo XIII titled: "On the New Things," *L. Rerum Novarum*).[1] This Papal Letter attempts to deal with workers' rights and the correlation between persons, systems, structures, institutions, and government. Instead of providing answers to complex socio-economic, and political questions or providing a roadmap, it seeks moreover to provide a theological framework which could open a discussion between the church and the world. It seeks to reform society and ultimately enhance the dignity of human persons under a more just social order. In addressing the dignity of the human person, it has a special emphasis on social justice for the poor and vulnerable in society. In CST, this would later be called "Preferential Option for the Poor."[2] In many ways social conditions are very different than those in 1891. However, poverty, injustice, oppression, and a disregard for the dignity of persons and their rights still exists in society, and in many ways, are far worse than they were a century ago.

In *Rerum Novarum*[3] we also find the first mention of distributive justice which will evolve through all the subsequent Papal Social Encyclicals and develop an understanding of a potential new economic system called "Distributism"[4] which speaks against the dangers of unfettered Capitalism as well as creating a basis for the condemnation of Socialism and Communism. This new system attempts to create a just balance between the people in society and the state, one which is based on distributive justice. With this Papal Letter began an articulation of the social dimension of Catholic thought which would gradually be put together in a systematic manner to ultimately be called CST and would be threaded throughout most of the future Papal Social Letters which would follow it. This social dimension of Catholic thought would additionally be incorporated into some of the Documents of Vatican Council II and several Bishop Synod Documents.[5]

CST is one of the best answers to the many problems which beset us in society to-day. It promotes virtue and discourages vice and gives preference to generosity and self-sacrifice over greed, self-interest, and power- mongering. It upholds social and economic justice and promotes family and community. It will even enable us to speak truth to power so that we might stand against unjust systems, structures, and institutions. Finally, it seeks to inspire in us a love and just concern for each other in society and especially the poor, lowly, weak, and oppressed because they are preferred by our Lord Jesus Christ who loved them first.

ROOTS IN SACRED SCRIPTURE

Although CST as a body of Catholic Doctrine had its formal beginning in history with Pope Leo's Letter, *Rerum Novarum*[6] in 1891, its roots can be traced back through the Tradition to find its earliest ground in the Sacred Scriptures thousands of years ago. The Bible clearly shows that God has been present, living, and active in human history. Here, from the very beginnings of Judeo-Christianity, is found the love of neighbor which is an expression of our love of God (Lv. 19: 9-18; Dt. 10:17; 30).[7] The human person is seen to have an inherent natural dignity, because he or she is made in the image and likeness of God (Gen. 1:27).[8] Because of this, there is found a call for justice in society, continuing up through the Old Testament Prophets. The call for social justice not only concerns loving our neighbor, but has a special emphasis on changing the structures that oppress people and particularly keep the poor, weak, and vulnerable in poverty. This is viewed as an outright attack on their human dignity because we are all made in God's image (Jer. 7:5-7, 22:13-16; Is. 1:16-17). Echoes of this refrain concerning God's love for the poor, lowly, and oppressed can also be found repeatedly in the Old Testament Psalms (Ps. 37:14, 40:18, 41:3, 69:34, 72:12, 86:1, 112:9, 113:7) and the Wisdom literature as well (Pvb.14:31, 17:5, 19:17; Job 29:12, 34:20-28; Sir. 4: 1-8, 21:3).[9]

In continuing into New Testament times, the love of neighbor can again be reaffirmed as a dimension of our love for God (Mt. 19:19; 22:39; Mk. 12:31-33; Lk. 10:27-29). It is particularly highlighted in the parable of the Good Samaritan as we are asked, "Who was neighbor to the man?" Here Jesus turns around the question of "Who is my neighbor?" by asking a much different and deeper question: "Who are you?" (Lk. 10:33-36). Who we consider as our neighbor goes to the very heart of our character and identity. The Apostle Paul also reaffirms love of neighbor as a dimension of our love for God (Rom. 13:9; Gal. 5:14). James discusses it as well in James 2:8.[10]

Themes of social justice appear 229 times in the Old Testament and are discussed another 67 times in the New Testament, with an emphasis particularly on justice for the poorest, weakest, and most vulnerable in society (Mt. 19:21; Mk. 10:21, 12:42; Lk. 18:1-22, 21:1-5; 2 Cor. 9:9; Gal. 2:1-10; Jam. 2:1-6). In fact, Jesus comes to "proclaim Good News to the poor" (Mt. 11:5; Lk. 4:18, 7:22).[11]

Any society can be judged on how well or how poorly it treats the poorest and most vulnerable. In societies marked with great division between the wealthy and the poor, we in the Judeo-Christian Tradition are called to oppose those structures, systems, and institutions which perpetuate this divide and should attempt to root out the abuses which create this oppression (Job 34:20; Is. 58:5-7). Our Christian faith demands justice for all. Therefore, any just economy whether it existed in early biblical times or today should serve the needs of all people in it, not just the few. Respect for the human dignity of each person, should dictate which economic structures, systems, and institutions serve people and insure that situations are not created where people end up serving the economy. Further, we should be in solidarity with one another and with the people of God throughout the ages. We should not be divided by systems and structures which perpetuate racial, ethnic, economic, ideological, or national division. The Apostle Paul tells us that we should seek to become: "one body in the Lord" (Rom. 12:5; 1 Cor. 12:12-27). The Scriptures and our Tradition also call us to: "Read the signs of the times," then to: "Observe, judge, and act."[12]

Chapter Two

Human Dignity; Love of God and Neighbor

HUMAN DIGNITY

Human dignity is an individual's or a group's sense of sacredness, respect, value, worth, integrity, and empowerment, extended to every person in society. God's love for all of us is the foundation of human dignity which is the bedrock of CST which proclaims at its core, "people before things." Our dignity naturally flows from our being and not our doing and has only to do with who we are human persons. It is essential to our humanity and inalienable. It is both personal and universal, and must be independent of one's character and conduct. All persons are created in the image and likeness of God (Gen. 1:27).[1] Because all people are created in God's image, all human life must be considered sacred from conception to natural death and respect for the inherent worth and value of every person in society should be embraced and flow from this. Man exists as a unique, intelligent, and conscious being, capable of self-understanding, self-possession and self-determination.

The transcendent dignity of each of us is realized in community with others. It is the criterion against which all aspects of economic life should be measured. All human beings, therefore, are the cause and end to be served by the institutions, systems, and governing bodies that make up the economy and not the means to be oppressed or exploited for narrow economic goals of the society. Human persons with their inherent dignity, because they are transcendent and made in the image of God, must particularly have the right to religious freedom and be free from coercion by the state to go against one's conscience in seeking the truth found ultimately in God. Everyone has a soul; therefore, the transcendent dignity of each must be recognized, preserved, and defended whenever and wherever necessary. Because we are by our very nature, transcendent creatures, every person must always be recognized as the principle, subject, and object of every social organization. A part of this transcendent human dignity which exists in man is our free will. This can be good or bad for others in society. This is because we can choose to serve God and others in society through the gifts and talents we are given, or we can pervert virtue into vice and attempt to get others in society to serve us in a slave-like fashion.

By and through the Incarnation of Jesus Christ, God, in a certain way has united Godself with each person who has equal dignity with every other, because before God, we are all radically equal. In Part 3; Q4; art. 5 of his *Summa,* Thomas Aquinas states, "...as He is the first-born of all creatures according to the Divine, for then all men would be of equal dignity."[2] Background, intelligence, race, gender, religion, economic status, nationality, or age can neither increase nor decrease any person's basic human dignity. The order of things must in all instances become subordinate to the order of persons and not the other way around. Excessive economic and social disparity between members of the one human race is a source of scandal and militates against human dignity.

A just society can only become a reality when it is based on this foundation. Whatever denigrates basic human dignity, such as inhumane living conditions, forms of slavery and prostitution, human trafficking; deplorable work environments, or any form of using people strictly for profit must never be tolerated in society. Where there is a human, there is being. Being begets goodness, truth, and beauty in the eyes of God and thus becomes a mandate for the dignity of all persons within the social order. Even when society might not fully recognize the dignity of persons in it and not be particularly just, the church, as the people of God, must be there in the breach to defend, promote, and safeguard the dignity of each and all.

LOVE OF GOD AND NEIGHBOR

We cannot come in touch with the divinity of God without touching humanity. Charity is the theological virtue that empowers us to love our neighbor. It is Jesus himself who calls us to "Love God with all our heart, soul, mind, and strength," and "Love our neighbor as our self (Lk. 10:25-27)." Jesus Christ's call to love God and neighbor was rooted in the divine revelation to the Israelite community which was embodied in the Torah (Dt. 6:5; Lv. 19:18).[3] If we cannot love the neighbor we see, how can we love the God we cannot see? Further, we cannot really love our neighbor unless we first respect their human dignity. To do this, the Holy Spirit must empower us to truly see the neighbor as another "self." Justice is a crucial part of the love of neighbor. When social or economic justice is lacking, neither love of God nor love of the neighbor can be present. Social or economic justice in any community can only be found when the persons in society respect the transcendent dignity not only of God, but of their neighbor as well.

The etymology of the word "neighbor" is from an old Anglo-Saxon word *neah* which meant "near."[4] With many rapid advances in technology, transportation and communication, the world is becoming a smaller and smaller place and all people regardless of nationality, race, creed, religion, or ethnicity can be seen today as "near." There exists today, a global interdependence. Seeing more people in society truly as our neighbor does not immediately change who they are, but it radically can change who we are.

In the ancient world, Jews hated Samaritans. The Jews of Jesus' society considered the Samaritans to be ceremonially unclean, socially outcast, and complete religious heretics. For the parable of The Good Samaritan in Luke 10:33-36[5] to make more sense for us today, we would have to change the title of it so that it could render the same message. Today the parable would have to be called something like the parable of "The Good Muslim." This is not to say that it would be right for any Christian to hate a Muslim; it's not. I use this only as a comparison because there are people in society today who do not immediately recognize a Muslim as their neighbor. Like the unselfish Samaritan of Jesus' parable, we are called to extend our love and social concern to all persons everywhere, as our neighbors. We should not exclude anyone or any group because of religious differences, social status, racial or ethnic difference or nationality.

In the end, we will all be judged by our response to Jesus who is present, embodied, and manifested in the neighbor in need. The Gospel poses this question of the love of neighbor for us:

> Lord, when did we see you hungry and feed you, or thirsty and give you drink? When did we see you a stranger and welcome you, or naked and clothe you? When did we see you ill or in prison and visit you? And the King will say to them in reply, 'Amen, I say to you, whatever you did for one of these least brothers and sisters of mine, you did for Me (Mt. 37:40).[6]

This parable has always made me shudder in my spirit every time I read it because Jesus does not say, "someone like me." He says, "you did for Me."

Chapter Three

Family and Community; Social and Economic Justice

FAMILY AND COMMUNITY

Our Triune God is social and is a communion/community of persons, Father, Son, and Holy Spirit. Therefore, we are called to be social and communal. There does exist a resemblance between the unity of persons in the Trinity and the family/community that men and women are called to establish among ourselves in love. Because the human person is both sacred and social we are called to protect each person's dignity not only in our family, but in the community as well. From the respect for each person's dignity and the love of our neighbor should flow our interdependence on each other and a desire to commit ourselves to the common good.

The family is the most basic social structure and is the first place where children begin to experience the need for community within the whole of society. It has rightly been called "the domestic church," as by its nature, it is a "sanctuary of life."[1] Children experience family as the first social order and the first community. The family, as a community of persons, is thus the first human society and the primary vital cell.

In the modern world, family is a term constituted with meaning because the meaning has experienced profound and rapid change over time. The structure of the family has come under attack particularly. It is within the family that a child first learns to be virtuous. Any single parent or any set of parents by their word and example should foster love not only within the immediate family, but should impart to their children a respect for the dignity of all human persons as an extended human family. They should develop a love of God and neighbor, and a desire for social justice to include a concern for the poorest and most vulnerable in society. Children who have been taught this will not only seek their own good, but will seek the good for all persons. The family, being a school for social life, will give birth to the interpersonal relationships that flow out into the broader community. The future of humanity and life in community must pass through the family unit.

Community is the extended family and consists of those people who are in communion with one another. Together they seek the common good of each member and have a common purpose and common goals. The good of any individual in a group or family unit is necessarily related to the common good, which in turn can only be defined in relation to each human person. The common good can be defined as: "The sum total of social conditions which allow people, either as groups or as individuals, to reach their fulfillment more fully and more easily." This presupposes respect for the dignity of the human person as such. In the name of the common good, public authorities are bound to respect the fundamental and inalienable rights of each human person.

The community requires the social well-being and development of all individuals in the group. Accessibility should be given to each in terms of what is needed to lead a truly human life: food, clothing, shelter, health, work, education and culture, the right to establish a family, etc. The community also requires the stability and security of a just social order with allowances for legitimate personal and collective defenses of the group. The world is made up of a family of families. The unity and solidarity of the human family, embracing people who enjoy equal natural dignity, implies a universal common good. This calls for an organization of the community of nations which provides for the necessities of life to alleviate the miseries of the poor and needy and their families.

Finally, the common good is always oriented towards the progress and development of persons. Any order of things must be subordinate to the order of persons, and not the other way around. While society often rewards and prizes individual achievement, CST states that human persons grow best and achieve fulfillment in community. How society is organized in economics and politics structurally within community will then directly affect the human dignity of each person and empower them to grow best in community. Persons have a right and a duty to participate in society, as they seek together the common good and well-being of all, especially the poorest and most vulnerable within the broader community. This approach to seeking the common good of all in society and being in "communion" should never be confused with Communism as an extreme state sponsored collectivist approach and one which is directly opposed by CST. The priority of the family over society and over the State must always be affirmed as the family does not exist for society or the State, but society and the State must exist for the family.

SOCIAL AND ECONOMIC JUSTICE

Society should seek to preserve and protect the human dignity and the basic rights of all individuals who are in it. Charitable works can meet the immediate needs of families and people in the broader community by responding to individual situations. However, social justice attempts to change the structures and institutions which oppress people, attack human dignity, and perpetuate cycles of poverty. Social justice defends the human rights of persons and works for social, political, and economic change over time. In a society where economic justice exists, moral principles will allow for the building of economic institutions and structures whose goal is to create opportunities for each person in the society to lead a dignified and productive life which enhances not only their individual existence, but also contributes to the common good.

Structures, systems, and institutions are meant to serve people. The economy, for example, should exist to serve the needs of the people in it. People should not exist simply to serve the economy. Because human persons are the cause and end of any social system or economy, there can be no complete social or economic justice unless it extends to all persons within the society and the furthest ends of any economy. This must include the poorest, weakest, and most vulnerable. Economic life should not revolve around the production and distribution of goods, or profit and power, but should rather be ordered to the service of persons in society and seek to foster social justice. All economic exchanges between people should always demand respect for the dignity of every human person involved in the economic exchanges.

Income inequality is a world- wide problem. However, when industrialized nations are compared, the United States is the most disparate. The difference is more glaring as 90% of the wealth in America is controlled by 10% of the families.[2] The gap between rich and poor has increased dramatically in the past decade. Many have now fallen below the poverty line and are being cut off from the distribution of wealth and full participation in the social, economic, and political life of our society. This renders them powerless and is no less than an assault on the human dignity of many people.

Social justice requires that people be assured a minimum level of participation in the economy. The way social, economic, and political institutions are organized, should foster economic and social justice and enable each person to participate in an active and productive life. What should be demanded of each person is to serve the common good and the well-being of all by insuring that the basic needs of every person are met. People should be asked to contribute to the economic and social life of the community in ways that respects their individual freedom and safeguards the dignity of their labor.

As regards CST, and its relation to social justice and economic activity, the Catholic Catechism (CC 2424-2449), as well as many of the modern Pope's Letters, Vatican Council II, and several Bishop's Pastoral Letters have spoken out against the systems, structures, and institutions in our modern day which continue to place things before people.[3] They have spoken out against Socialism and Communism on the one hand, condemning them and calling them, "totalitarian and atheistic ideologies;" which place the state before people. They also have spoken out strongly against unfettered Capitalism as a corrupted system which places money, profit and power before people and is governed by the laws of the marketplace. This undermines the basis of social bonds and works against the existence of social and economic justice as well as militates against human dignity and the common good. The scriptures tell us "You cannot serve God and money (Lk. 16:13)."[4] This does not imply that money in and of itself is evil, for it is the love of money which is evil. When people are placed before the marketplace, economic systems, structures, and institutions will then naturally become more *adjusted* (literal translation, "made right and just") socially and economically.

Any correct understanding of social and economic justice must allow for a distinction between society and the state. Society includes the complex dynamics of social, economic, political, religious, and cultural interrelationships to enhance the common good. The state is the center of civil authority and power by which these social purposes and interrelationships are to be preserved and this should be accomplished at the lowest level of intervention possible.

In reviewing many of the modern Papal Letters through which much of CST has evolved since 1891, you find the oft repeated call for more distributive justice in society. This concerns the nature of a socially just allocation and distribution of power, goods, and resources. It is considered unjust for anyone to appropriate surplus goods solely for their own private use when others lack the bare necessities of life. Socio-economic issues will always overlap with moral behavior. This makes the church's social doctrine and the relevant thought contained in it not simply a study of economics or of social thought, but of theology, and particularly moral theology.

Finally, it should be stated that anyone who ventures to speak to people about any kind of justice, must first be considered just in their eyes or it will become just "windy words."

Chapter Four

Rights and Duties; Socialization, Solidarity and Subsidiarity

RIGHTS AND DUTIES

Justice is a cornerstone on which any society should be built. The English word "justice" is derived from the Latin word "*ius*" which means "right."[1] By definition, a right is any person's moral claim upon other persons or upon society. In this sense, rights are discerned from the duties and responsibilities we owe one another as human beings created in God's image. Justice then, is that virtue which perfects the will and inclines it to render to each and all what belongs to them by right. A right then, is a power we have, to do things in society for the benefit of all persons in society. It is also a moral claim upon other persons or upon society to empower one to reach that destiny which is theirs. These rights are universal, inalienable and indivisible. They apply to every stage of life from birth to death and to every social, political, economic and cultural situation. They are the minimum conditions for life in community.

Vatican Council II has given us an idea of what constitutes a human right. Pope John Paul II has reaffirmed them in his modern letter, (The One Hundredth Year), *Centesimus Annus* written on the 100th anniversary of the first letter of CST written in 1891, which was (On the New Things), *Rerum Novarum*.[2] These human rights are outlined as:

1. The right to life which is an integral part of the right of the child to develop in the mother's womb from the moment of conception and to continue to life's natural end.

2. The right to live in a united family and in a moral environment conducive to the growth of the child's personality.
3. The right to develop one's intelligence and freedom in seeking and knowing the truth.
4. The right to share in the work which makes wise use of the earth's material resources, and to derive from that work the means to support oneself and one's dependents.
5. The right freely to establish a family, to have and to rear children through the responsible exercise of one's sexuality.
6. The source and synthesis of these rights is religious freedom, understood as the right to live in the truth of one's faith and in conformity with one's transcendent dignity as a human person.
7. A right to respect for human dignity regardless of race, creed, gender, religion, or nationality.

Our role is to "ad-just" within society to accomplish the giving of these rights to each person for the benefit of the common good. The proclamation of human rights is one of the most significant attempts to respond positively to the demands of human dignity. Human dignity can only be protected in society if human rights are protected and responsibilities of all human beings in society are met.

Rights and duties are interrelated in every social and political activity of man. Rights flow from duties. In human society, one man's right, corresponds to a duty in all other persons. That duty constitutes simply the acknowledgment and respect for the right in question.

Christian righteousness requires that we live in a way that is consistent with the death and resurrection of Jesus Christ and his gift of salvation. From this should flow our duties to one another as members of the body of Christ. In a society where there is perfect Christian love, any question of rights and duties would then become moot. We are surely a long way from this.

SOCIALIZATION, SOLIDARITY, AND SUBSIDIARITY

Society is the way we organize ourselves and consists of a complex network of social, political, economic, cultural and religious relationships which are necessary for full human participation and development. CST maintains that the human person should always be the principle, subject and object of every social organization. Socialization expresses the natural tendency for human beings to associate with one another for the sake of attaining objectives that exceed individual capacities. It is this interdependence of persons in society which gives rise to patterns of group life and behavior and to resulting social organizations, structures and institutions. Further, it is the process whereby an individual learns to adjust to a community (or within society). It also refers to the process by which social norms, customs or values could provide persons in community with the skills and habits necessary for participating in the life of a community (or within society).

One of the ways social justice can be achieved in any community is through finding the right balance between solidarity and subsidiarity. Both have their respective roles in the Catholic understanding of community as a communion of people. We are all in this together, and there exists a common need for us to be each other's keeper. Solidarity is about valuing the basic human dignity and rights of those in community and learning to respect who they are as individuals. It is a spirit of unity, whereby we are bonded with one another; including and especially the poorest, weakest, and most vulnerable in society. Solidarity is the glue that bonds us. It emphasizes social charity, participation, and mutual support by persons in community. Furthermore, it views interdependence as something very beneficial to society and as something which should be cherished by all. CST maintains that solidarity has two complimentary aspects, that of social principle and that of moral virtue. It is as a moral virtue in that it determines the order of social institutions. Structures, systems, and institutions which are unjust, sinful, and evil should be identified, dismantled, transformed, and then replaced with those of solidarity. In its insistence upon seeking the good of every individual in a group, it will result in making a firm commitment to the common good. It is then as a virtue which stresses a commitment to the common good that solidarity becomes a fundamental social virtue, as it then places itself in the realm of the cardinal virtue of justice. Some things that work against solidarity in society are injustice, oppression, prejudice, intolerance, greed, fear, selfishness, exploitation, exclusion, marginalization, a disregard for life and the structure of the family unit, and a basic lack of love and concern for the well-being of our neighbor. Although all persons in society may not embrace being Christian, Jesus Christ is still at the center and heart of our solidarity with God and each other through his incarnation. Jesus' solidarity with all of humanity makes it far more powerful and mystical than mere fellowship. It truly makes us not only "Catholic," in a religious sense, but "Universal" as one body in Christ.

While solidarity refers to the unity of the whole body; subsidiarity refers to the role of the respective parts of the body. Subsidiarity establishes and maintains a delicate relationship between individual initiative and governmental direction, while charting a course between individualism and collectivism. It emphasizes the transfer of responsibility and authority and suggests that nothing should be done at a higher level which can be done at a lower or more local level, assuming of course, that the lowest level is compatible with the common good.

Both solidarity and subsidiarity should always be maintained in as much of a balance as possible. Perfect balance is not always easy and this may require some in the community to speak and act for greater social and economic justice, especially for the poorest, weakest and most vulnerable. It may further necessitate speaking out against unjust systems, structures and institutions. When the principle of subsidiarity is ignored, government will very often overstep its bounds in managing matters best handled at a lower or more local level. This will lead to government infringing upon the rights of individuals and groups in society to dominate rather than to serve them. Typically, this will decrease economy, efficiency will suffer, bureaucracy will flourish, and freedom will be constrained. Ultimately, the personal character of the social order will be disrupted and often negated. It was President Abraham Lincoln who once said in his Presidential address:

> The legitimate object of government is to do for a community of people whatever they need to have done, but cannot do at all or cannot do so well for themselves — in their separate and individual capacities.[3]

Chapter Five

The Role of Government; Preferential Option for the Poor

THE ROLE OF GOVERNMENT

Any government should recognize first that the power to rule and to govern comes from God and is a participation in God's sovereignty. Furthermore, that every human life which lives and breathes in each citizen of the state is precious in the eyes of God. This makes persons more sacred than any property governed by the state. Government therefore, must protect and defend the basic human dignity of all.

We are social beings; consequently, the state is natural to the person and has a positive moral function. The state and its governors have a duty to make sure that the laws and institutions and the general character of the administration should always promote human dignity, defend and protect human rights, pursue justice in society, promote public well-being, defend the interests of the most vulnerable and contribute to the edification of the common good. The state also has a duty to assist citizens in fulfilling their responsibility to others in society. In any large society, these responsibilities cannot necessarily be carried out on a one-to-one basis. Therefore, citizens need the help of government to promote the common good. The principle of Subsidiarity, a central tenet of CST, states that government should be as small as possible and only as big as necessary.

Citizens are free to choose whatever form of government they please, provided there exists a proper regard for justice and the common good. The justification of all government action should be the common good. Governments engaged in boosting society and the world's economy should always be considerate of the fact that the primary capital to be safeguarded and valued is the human person in his or her integrity. As was stated at Vatican

Council II: "Man is the source, the focus and the aim of all economic and social life (Vat. II, GS# 63)."[1]

Laws passed in contravention of the moral order and hence of the divine will can have no binding force in conscience, since it is right to obey God rather than men. Any laws which government passes should promote justice and well-being for all citizens and not give preference to the wealthy or any business, regardless of size. Government should recognize that every person has a right to participate in the just distribution of goods and resources. It should also recognize that individuals have a right to possess private property. This must always have a social mortgage to protect the interests and inclusiveness of the poorest and weakest members of society. The general needs of human existence here modify the strict isolated definition of private property. The right to private property should always yield to a higher right, and that is the right of human beings to basic subsistence.

Government should always be democratic and participatory. It should not intrude or attempt to exercise intimate control over the lives of members of the family or the community. The more that individuals are defenseless within a given society the more they may require the care and concern of others, and particularly the intervention of governmental authority. In situations where families are experiencing extreme distress, they may request public assistance since the family is a vital part of the community. In defending and protecting the poorest in society, government should recognize that oftentimes the destruction of the environment can contribute to the heaviest impact on the poorest in society.

The human environment and the natural environment deteriorate together. Economic growth should be fostered by the government, with an eye to environmental and ecological deterioration. At all times, government should take measures to defend the proper functioning of the environment and to preserve precious resources. It should seek to counter all significant threats to the environment which would threaten or harm the very life of the members of society. It should develop laws, regulations, procedures, and controls to accomplish this. Environmental decisions may occasionally have both ecological and economic consequences. One type of decision should not take precedence over the other. Both should be given equal consideration by all levels of government.

PREFERENTIAL OPTION FOR THE POOR

The phrase "preferential option for the poor" was first used in 1968 by the superior general of the Jesuits, Father Pedro Arrupe, in a letter to his order.[2] The term was later used by Catholic bishops of South and then North America,[3] was widely utilized recently by many modern Catholic theologians and then appeared of late in the Social Letters of the last three Popes; John Paul II, Benedict XVI, and Francis[4] Preference for the poor, however, has a history in the Judeo-Christian Tradition which is much older than that and is solidly rooted in the Old and New Testaments of the Bible (EX. 22:20-26; LV. 19:9-10; JB. 34:20-28; PR. 31:8-9; IS. 25:4-5, 58:5-7; MT. 25:34-40; LK. 4:16-21, 6:20-23). As Jesus said, "The Poor are with you always, but you will not always have me (MT 26:11)."[5] This should never be read as a prediction; but only as a comparison. God certainly does not want to keep the poor in poverty, but they are with us as a sign and sacrament of his presence among us. For any Catholic, the commitment to the poor as sign and sacrament of his presence among us, arises from an experience of Christ in the Eucharist. As the Catholic Catechism teaches us: "To receive in truth the Body and Blood of Christ given up for us, we must recognize Christ in the poorest... (CC no. 1397)."[6]

Because there currently exists a wide diversity of social and economic situations in which Christians find themselves according to regions, socio-political systems, and cultures, very often the poor are unwillingly kept on the fringes of society. When the words, "preferential option for the poor" are used, it may seem that CST is siding with poorer people in opposition to those who are wealthy. In some senses, this is true because it is poorer people who are more often in need of an advocate. The wealthy have the resources to be their own advocate or to hire advocates. To desire the common good and strive towards this goal is a requirement of justice and love. Therefore, it may be even better to say that the fundamental reason CST insists that a "preferential option for the poor" be made by society at large is because deprivation, oppression, marginalization and powerlessness of the poor ultimately ends up wounding the whole of the community. Further, if society doesn't make a "preferential option for the poor," then by default it makes "a preferential option for the status quo." Every society is judged on how it treats the poorest of the poor. Solidarity presupposes the effort for a more just social order which will be inclusive of the poorest, weakest, and most vulnerable. This is necessary not only because they have human dignity but because we are called to love our neighbor in the same way that we love God and ourselves. Radical inequalities and the unjust structures which perpetuate and support them are not only contrary to the Gospel, but also do not benefit the common good. Radical social disparity between individuals and peoples should only be viewed as simply scandalous.

When there exists a question of defending the rights of individuals, Catholics should speak for the voiceless and defend the defenseless. Those who are the poorest, weakest, and most vulnerable should and must be given special consideration. Because the poor very often do not possess resources of their own to depend upon, they must depend upon the occasional assistance of church missionary outreaches, private and volunteer organizations, and the government. However, the principles of solidarity and subsidiarity should be applied here. Dependence upon the government should only occur where necessary and should come from the lowest level possible whenever the need arises. This should not imply that government has the primary role, but it does have a positive moral responsibility in safeguarding human rights and ensuring that the minimum conditions of human dignity are met.

Although the principle of subsidiarity holds that larger institutions in society should not interfere with smaller or more local institutions, larger institutions do have essential responsibilities. These apply when the more local institutions cannot adequately protect the human dignity of poor persons, meet their human needs, or don't advance the common good. Solidarity without subsidiarity can easily degenerate into any society becoming a welfare state, while subsidiarity without solidarity fosters a climate of encouraging excessive and ineffective local control. To balance both principles the state's intervention in the economic environment should neither be too invasive nor should it be left wanting. It should always be commensurate with needs and in doing this, give preference to the needs of the poorest and most vulnerable.

Our response to the poor as Catholics, should not be assistance alone, but should encompass advocacy for social and economic change, speaking out against unjust systems and structures which oppress the poor and perpetuate cycles of poverty, and empowerment and support of economic development to raise their level of participation. In any economy, the creation of jobs and expanded employment is crucial. The goal of empowering the poor to be increasingly self-reliant should always be an economic and social horizon.

Vatican Council II in its *Pastoral Constitution on the Church* declared:

> The joys and hopes, the griefs and anxieties of the people of this age, especially those who are poor or in any way afflicted, these too are the joys and hopes, the griefs and anxieties of the followers of Christ (Vat II, GS #1).[7]

There is an ancient story in the Tradition of the Catholic Church concerning St. Lawrence, the third century deacon of Rome and the treasurer of the church's financial resources. The Emperor Valerian, had ordered a bloody persecution of Christians and soon demanded that St. Lawrence bring him the "riches of the church." St. Lawrence, who had already given these financial resources to the poor, brought all these poor people to Valerian at the Emperor's palace, telling him, "Here are the riches of the church."[8]

Chapter Six

Participation and Work; Freedom and Life

PARTICIPATION AND WORK

It is a moral obligation of society to be participative. Participation is a pillar of democracy which by its very nature must be as such. It is one of the chief characteristics of solidarity and is any activity by which a person as an individual or in a group contributes to the economic, cultural, and political life of the society. Participation is always fulfilled with an eye to the common good. It is impossible to promote the dignity of the person without concern for the family, groups, associations and other expressions to which people spontaneously give life and make it possible for them personally and communally to achieve effective social growth. How we organize our society in economics and politics, directly affects human dignity and the capacity of individuals to grow in community. Whenever we as Catholics, become caught up strictly in our own interests and desires, there is no longer room for others to participate and we allow no place in our hearts preferentially for the poor. Participation by its very nature should imply that everyone has a place in the community whether it is a community as small as the family structure or as large as the global village. Social Justice should imply that persons have an obligation to be active and productive participants in the ongoing life of the society. Society, on the other hand, has a duty and a responsibility to enable them to participate in this way.

Work is a form of participation in society, and it is a duty. From the beginning of time, work has been a part of man's role and a fundamental dimension of our existence on earth. Catholics understand further that all work should be done in the light of the creative plan of God. Essentially, we are participating in a sharing in the ongoing work of God and work honors the gifts and talents He has given to us. In this way, it can be redemptive. Therefore, our Catholic faith calls us to demand justice for all workers and to insist on a just economy that serves all. Furthermore, all workers have a right to productive work and have a right to participate in the economic and political life of the society. They also have a right to organize. Solidarity should exist between employers and employees and will manifest itself through the fair and just distribution of goods and in adequate remuneration for work. Conflicts in this regard should be settled by negotiation. It should always be considered that work is for man and not man for work, therefore a just wage is the legitimate fruit of that work.

It should also be recalled that the first CST Letter was written as recently as 1891 by Pope Leo XIII, (*Rerum Novarum*) and was subtitled "On the Conditions of Labor."[1] It was foundational and addressed the unjust conditions which oppressed the working classes. This Letter and its significance will be discussed later in Section II of this book, when all the Social Letters of the modern Popes will be individually discussed.

FREEDOM AND LIFE

Freedom through our God-given free will enables us to direct ourselves toward God and goodness. "To do" is an act of freedom which affects our becoming the person we were meant to be in the eyes of God. It is only in freedom that we can love God, our self, or any other person. It is a right to choose life, shape and perfect it, without externally imposed restraints, and as more than the inevitable outcome of our circumstances, heritage, and environment.

God's Providence occurs at the intersection of our free-will and the omnipotence of God and allows us to receive the offer of grace to take part in shaping our life, character, identity, and destiny. Through freedom and grace, we have the capacity in time, space, and history to choose who will be our final irrevocable self in this life. It is at the heart of what it means to be human and doesn't as much allow us to do something as to be someone. Because freedom can be exaggerated and corrupted and become the vice of license there must be limits to our freedom when it infringes on the lives of another human person's freedom. These limits may be self-imposed through conscience and the virtue of temperance. They may also be outwardly imposed through our experience of self in religious and social community or the rule of law within the church and society (ex. Our personal freedom to swing our arm in the air stops at the point of our neighbor's nose).

Freedom can also tend toward license when it involves the taking of another human life, such as in matters involving abortion or euthanasia. These matters of freedom and life become particularly problematic because church law may occasionally conflict today with civil law. The question of religious freedom is specifically discussed in the Vatican II document, "Declaration on Religious Freedom," *Dignitatis Humanae.*[2] Most of the Papal Social Letters of the past 100+ years will address the question of freedom and life in not only its spiritual dimension, but in its economic, social, and political dimensions as well. The dynamic of freedom and life becomes most evident in the Social Letters of Pope John Paul II, particularly in "The Gospel of Life," *Evangelium Vitae.*[3]

Chapter Seven

The Marketplace and Consumerism; Respect for God's Creation— The Environment

THE MARKETPLACE AND CONSUMERISM

The marketplace is a "thing," and too often has been given precedence to the rights of workers who are people. This violates one of the basic tenets of CST, which once again, is, "people before things." One of the major issues which should concern us as Catholics participating in a free market economy is that we have reached a point where we don't interact with each other as much as we interact with the marketplace. This has led to excessive consumerism. Consumerism is based on economic policies which emphasize consumption. People begin to identify more with the products and services they consume than with one another. In many ways we have become like, "the children of the marketplace who call to one another," which Jesus refers to in Matthew's Gospel (Mt. 11:16-18).

With so called, "conspicuous consumption," people seek only to satisfy their wants and desires. Thus, we become "thingafied" and often don't realize it. This creates situations which result in lavish spending on goods and services which are acquired mainly for displaying income, extravagance, social power, and wealth. Practical utility of goods and services is no longer operative as acquisition supplants this and becomes the organizing principle of the free market economy. The production of voracious consumers becomes the major product of a consumerist economy as people are turned into desiring-machines, always wanting more. This all feeds an endless need to expand the economy and to eat up more and more of our ecosystems in the process.

Excessive consumerism always has a distant moving target to keep its adherents spending money. Because billions are spent on advertising and marketing to fan the flames of our desires, increasing ease of access to available credit, no one in an excessive consumption society is exempt from its temptation. A societal plague of behavioral addiction has broken out and unfortunately it continues to spread its contagion. Society becomes numb and consequently little thought is given to the fact that all this might be occurring at the expense of other people near and far. Some are living with much more than they need, so others have little or nothing at all. The culture of materialism which surrounds all this reshapes our desires and makes them appear acceptable, natural, and normal. It redirects our God-given passions to things that can never ultimately make us happy or fulfill us and moves us away from a spiritually based community in solidarity with one another. But, God is not on sale at our nearest department store. God is in our family, in our neighbor and in our poorest brother and sister, both near and far. The emptier our heart is, the more we desire and feel a need for things to buy, possess, and consume. As Augustine said long ago, "Lord, our hearts are restless, until they can find rest in you."[1]

In the final analysis, increasing the consumption of resources which is based more on wants than needs to satisfy the increasing demands of the marketplace, can only lead to that which is beyond environmental sustainability. Ultimately, it will lead to destruction of the ecosystem.

RESPECT FOR GOD'S CREATION-THE ENVIRONMENT

The earth produces enough resources to meet all our needs, but it does not produce enough to meet all our wants. Consuming less and in a more conscious manner would save a vast amount of the world resources. We are stewards of God's creation therefore we are called to respect the goods and the gifts of the earth. It is the only common home we know, and we must preserve it for coming generations. The whole human race suffers because of environmental blight, and generations yet unborn will bear the cost for our failure to act today.

Conspicuous consumption and the unnecessary production of goods that feeds it is far and away the biggest contributor to global environmental destruction. A child born in a developed country, for example, puts a far heavier burden on the planet's resources than one born in a poor and undeveloped country. Environmental problem issues such as greenhouse gases, pollution, soil erosion, water shortages, forest destruction, rising tides, global warming and climate change can be tied directly or indirectly to the excess consumption of goods and services. This is not to mention the several economic issues that perpetuate cycles of poverty that can be tied to it. Without constant and burgeoning consumption, the environment would have the time it requires to replenish the resources it provides for us. In the past fifty years, for example, people on the planet have consumed more in the way of goods produced than all the people who have come before us in history.

CST brings a new perspective to the issues of the environment by simply not presenting them as environmental issues only. For these issues are, in effect, moral issues and economic issues as well. It is morally challenging in that CST calls us to examine how we truly love our neighbor, have concern for the poor, and use and share the goods of the earth, as well as what we will pass on to future generations. First and foremost, these environmental issues, like many economic issues, affect the poor, weak, and vulnerable of society and hit them the hardest.

Issues such as pollution, food and water shortages, climate change, and conflicts over declining resources affect those on the margins before they affect anyone else. Our love for God, our neighbor, the poor, and the environment cannot be separated. Further on in this book when we examine Pope Francis' letter on the environment, *Laudato Si,* which is now a part of CST, he states emphatically: "The poor and the earth are crying out." As well as: "There is an intimate relationship between the poor and the fragility of the planet" (LS, no. 16).[2]

Many who read Pope Francis' Letter, *Laudato Si,* (translated as "Praise Be") wondered what gave him the right to speak out on economy and ecology together as they seemed unrelated and should be separate issues. Furthermore, they don't seem directly related to church issues. But, the two words are related even at their root, as eco means "dwelling place." This would make ecology part of the story of our dwelling place. *Oikonomos, (Gk)* from which comes the word "economy" is translated as a "household manager."[3] So, the Holy Father probably saw himself as speaking out as the simple head of a household which is our dwelling place. In this case the household is the entire people of God who live in the dwelling place and share the planet as our common home. God, alone has a dwelling place extending to the entire universe. As God's people, we shouldn't have to choose between people and the planet because they are the same choice.

In speaking out on the dangers of unfettered or unrestrained Capitalism, Pope Francis warns in his Encyclical, The Joy of the Gospel," *Evangelii Gaudium*:

> In this system, which tends to devour everything which stands in the way of increased profits, whatever is fragile, like the environment, is defenseless before the interests of a deified market, which becomes the only rule (EG #56).[4]

This would also say in many respects that there is a link between natural ecology and human ecology and that socio-economic and environmental issues are directly connected. Although Pope Francis never said so explicitly, this link between people and the planet might even go so far as to indicate that between men, there can be no peace on earth until there is peace with the earth.

Chapter Eight

Evangelization-Come Holy Spirit

After Jesus of Nazareth was crucified and rose from the dead, he promised to have the Father send the Holy Spirit (Jn. 14:15-31). The themes of CST we've discussed thus far in this book are going to be virtually impossible to achieve without the Holy Spirit working with and within us. Unless the Holy Spirit is working to transform our hearts and then stirring other hearts to be receptive and willing to change systems, structures, and institutions, none of this will occur. We need more power than simply our own will power. We need the same power that created the universe which is dwelling within us. The Lord, through the Holy Spirit dwelling within us wishes to accomplish his will on earth by using us to do his will. As we are told in the Scriptures: "Unless the Lord builds the house, the builders labor in vain (Ps. 127:1)."

Spirit-filled evangelizing means evangelizers fearlessly open to the working of the Holy Spirit, for, how can we truly love our neighbor, if we don't even really like him? Or how can we change unjust systems, structures, and institutions, or reverse environmental blight which threatens life on the planet if the people responsible for these decisions are unreceptive? Lifting the poor out of poverty, bringing about social and economic justice, having society begin to put people before things-all of these are impossible without the Holy Spirit. It will only be possible because the Holy Spirit, who is "the spirit of truth," will be our guide (Jn. 16:3).[1] Only the Spirit can enable us to speak truth to power.

Pope Francis has called us to embark on a "new chapter of evangelization marked by joy." To do this we must take on the "smell of the sheep."[2] Each of us, by virtue of our baptism, has the sanctifying power of the Holy Spirit at work in us, impelling us to evangelize. We are social and relational beings: first in relation to God through the Holy Spirit, then through the Holy Spirit in relation to neighbor and the world. To live in Christian community is to be in the presence of the Holy Spirit who has the power to transform the world.

In the ancient Christian community, they spoke Greek and the Bible was written in Greek. The Greek word the writers used for spirit was *dynamis*[3] which implied a strong inherent power residing in something or someone. From *dynamis* we get our modern English words "dynamic" and "dynamite." If the Holy Spirit is in us we will not only be dynamic, but exploding with evangelical enthusiasm and bursting with joy as we go out into the world in the power of the Spirit. We will be able to live out the words of Isaiah as Jesus did when he unrolled the scroll and spoke them long ago in the temple: "The Spirit of the Lord is upon me…God has anointed me to bring glad tidings to the poor…to proclaim liberty to captives… to let the oppressed go free (Lk. 4:18)."[4]

The Holy Spirit acts in every evangelizer who is led by the Spirit. Because it is the role of the Holy Spirit to first renew us and then to renew the face of the earth, every form of authentic evangelization is always 'new'. The primary reason for evangelizing is the love of Jesus. Therefore, there can be no proclamation of the Gospel and no true evangelization without the explicit proclamation of 'Jesus as Lord.' Jesus Christ has primacy in all evangelizing work.

To evangelize is to make the Kingdom of God present in our world. Therefore, we should also be conscious of the fact that there is most often a social dimension of evangelization. The task of evangelization demands first that we recognize that this is the work of the Holy Spirit, not our work. Then it demands recognition of the transcendent dignity in every human being. We must also recognize that evangelization has a social dimension because the Lord redeems not only the individual person, but also the social relations existing between people. Furthermore, to renew the face of the earth, the Holy Spirit may not want to simply change people, but may also want to transform many of the systems, structures and institutions which marginalize, oppress, or impoverish people.

As Catholics, the prayer, *Come Holy Spirit,*[5] is one which should always be on our lips if we truly hear the immense challenges that CST is asking of us as we seek out our role in evangelization and try to bring about change and renewal. First, we must become the change we want to see. Our own lives need to be changed and transformed by the Holy Spirit. We are all called as Catholics to reflect deeply on the events unfolding before our eyes in the world and to respond to them out of mature faith. We should first be praying, *Come, Holy Spirit,* while asking the Holy Spirit to be our guide. Then we should always be "reading the signs of the times" (Mt 16:3) as Jesus asks of us in the Gospels. Lastly, we should put our Catholic social principles into action by "observing, judging, and acting" as CST asks of us (*MM* # 236).[6]

Holy Spirit Prayer: *Come Holy Spirit*

Come Holy Spirit, fill the hearts of your faithful and kindle in them the fire of your love.

Send forth your Spirit and they shall be created. And You shall renew the face of the earth.

O, God, who by the light of the Holy Spirit, did instruct the hearts of the faithful, grant that by the same Holy Spirit we may be truly wise and ever enjoy His consolations, Through Christ Our Lord, Amen.

Holy Spirit Hymn: *Come Holy Ghost*

Come, Holy Ghost, Creator blest,
and in our hearts, take up Thy rest;
come with Thy grace and heavenly aid
to fill the hearts which Thou hast made.[7]

AUTHOR'S NOTE

What follows in Section Two is an analysis of the modern Papal Social Letters/Encyclicals beginning with Pope Leo's XIII's foundational Letter, "On the New Things," (*Rerum Novarum*), written in1891.[8] This Letter was the beginning of the formation of Catholic Social Teaching as it exists today. The Papal Letters included after *Rerum Novarum* in Section Two follow every Social Encyclical of every Pope up through Pope Francis', "Praise Be," (*Laudato Si*), written in 2015.[9] The "Themes of CST," which were just outlined in the first part of this book can be traced to the Bible and Tradition of the Church, but are mostly threaded throughout all the Papal Social Letters which now follow. For the purposes of this book and its material I tried to focus on every facet of CST in the Papal Letters in comprising these themes. However, I paid attention particularly to what each of the Pope's Social Letters had to say about distributive justice, or the lack of it in society. Distributive justice and Distributism as an economic theory will be the focus of Section Three, the final section of the book.

Section Two: Catholic Social Teaching and the Social Letters of the Modern Popes

Chapter Nine

On the New Things-(*Rerum Novarum*), Pope Leo XIII, 1891*

This Letter is more commonly referred to as, *On the Condition of the Working Classes,* as well as the title, *On Capital and Labor.* [1] It was the foundational Letter that began a new direction in Catholic Moral Theology, one that also began the formal basis of Catholic Social Teaching. With this Letter, the Catholic Church initiated a dialogue between the church and the modern world and established its social role as it began to boldly speak out on current and future matters of immense socio-economic concern.

In the mid 1800's many social revolutions erupted in countries across Europe. Much in the way of social and economic devastation had been the result of the Industrial Revolution. New Socialist, Communist, and Capitalist mindsets were stirring in society. By the late 1800's, Pope Leo XIII and the Catholic hierarchy saw much happening in the world that contributed to the diminishing of human dignity and the building of societies lacking in social and economic justice. What really moved Pope Leo to write the Letter was his conviction that the present age had handed over the working poor to inhumane employers and greedy competitors. He sought to protect the rights of workers and to speak out against the growth in power of state sponsored Socialist/Communist movements as well as speaking out against the growth of unrestricted Capitalism. The role of the church, the role of the state, and the role of associations were also established in the document.

In section #33 of the Letter, Pope Leo first refers to "Distributive Justice" as grounded in *the Summa* of Thomas Aquinas[2] after having previously discussed it in section # 24.[3]

Several subsequent papal Letters would refer to distributive justice as well and from this reference later Catholic theologians such as G.W. Chesterton would use the term "Distributism"[4] when referring to an untried economic theory while discussing economic justice in society.

The Letter sought to further establish mutual rights and duties between the rich and the poor, owners and workers, capital and labor. Pope Leo also sought to champion virtue and the right to private property over and against state ownership held in common. His Letter gave justification for putting persons and their inherent human dignity before any state. Further, it was stated that workers had the right to organize into mutual associations. Overall this Letter championed poor workers and spoke truth to power in stating that powerful systems, structures, institutions, and political states should not treat labor as if it was a commodity.

Much of the material discussed in this Letter would be referenced and shows up in many of the later modern Papal Letters which followed. For example, here we see the beginnings of many later discussions in more recent Papal Letters on areas like human dignity, workers' rights, family and community, social and economic justice, subsidiarity and the role of government, the condemnation of Socialism, Communism, and unrestrained Capitalism. We also get hints of what was to later come to be called "The Preferential Option for the Poor" in Catholic Social Teaching:[5]

God Himself seems to incline rather to those who suffer misfortune; for Jesus Christ calls the poor 'blessed"; (Mt.5:3) He lovingly invites those in labor and grief to come to Him for solace; (Matt. 11:28), and He displays the tenderest charity toward the lowly and the oppressed (RN # 24).[6]

Rerum Novarum truly was, as the translation from the Latin indicated "On the New Things." The Letter was revolutionary in many respects, but what was most radical, was that it certainly began the alignment of the Catholic Church with the poor, exploited, and oppressed of the world. It further established how the church wasn't simply on earth to save men's eternal souls, but also to address the temporal importance of socio-economic matters and putting people and their human dignity before things like systems, structures, institutions, and political states.

As Jesus tells us in the Gospels, "God is the God of the living not of the dead (Mt. 22:32-33)."[7] Because God is the God of the living and all are alive to Him, He is the Lord of history and the temporal and the eternal. He lives in both realms. Aristotle, Augustine, and Aquinas have all told us that the temporal and the eternal, though vastly different, are certainly connected and have much to do with each other.[8]

Beginning in 1891, the Catholic Church began to see its role on earth as not only saving men's eternal souls, but always, (present and future) to stand in the breach and defend God's poor, defenseless, and oppressed. It would begin to speak out boldly and plainly in the socio-economic/temporal realm. To do this effectively, the Catholic Church would have to evolve and truly become what it seemed destined to be, "The Church in the Modern World."

It would not call itself that, however, for another 74 years until Vatican Council II in 1965.[9]

This Letter can be found in its entirety at the Vatican Website: http: // w2.vatican.va/content/leo-xiii/en.html

*Ibid see endnote #1

Chapter Ten

On the Fortieth Year- (*Quadragesimo Anno*), Pius XI, 1931*

This Letter was written by Pius XI some ten years after being elected Pope and on the 40th anniversary of *Rerum Novarum*. It was subtitled, *On Reconstruction of the Social Order*. In the forty years that separated the writing of each letter, labor associations had grown but not to the extent that they could correct many of the injustices against workers. The centralization of wealth had become much more concentrated and the poor had become poorer. In America and much of the world, the Great Depression had come upon society. This Letter clearly placed the church in-line with those who had been arguing that economic activity must be regulated for the sake of the overall common good.

Pope Pius will be less defensive than Leo and will not so much defend the right of the Catholic Church to speak out on socio-economic issues as much as to say it is the God-given right, responsibility, and duty of the church to do that. It is assumed rather than open for debate. He saw his own purpose in writing this Letter primarily to reiterate many of the points made previously by Pope Leo on such matters as human dignity, rights of workers, defense of the poor, private property, associations, capital and labor, labor not being a commodity, and the role of government. The principle of Subsidiarity, which Pope Leo had raised in a skirted manner, first begins to be thoroughly formulated here in this Letter in more detail. (QA # 79-80)[1]

Throughout the Letter, on seven separate occasions, Pope Pius will talk about "inequality in the distribution of this world's goods," and "just distribution," (QA #5, 57, 58, 60, 61, 76, 136).[2] These are certainly his references to "distributive justice."

Pius also sought to combat some doubts that had arisen in society and the church concerning the force and validity of Leo's socio-economic thought and theology, but he will take a somewhat different approach than Pope Leo in that he will discuss specifically the ethical implications of the social and economic order. Because he believes that socio-economic issues will always overlap with moral behavior, he talks about a growing and developing body of Catholic social and economic thought. It was presently being studied in Catholic colleges, universities, and seminaries and he refers to it both as "Catholic Social Science" and "Catholic Philosophy." This will subsequently be referred to as Catholic Social Teaching by many who follow him.

Pope Pius admits in the letter that it will be virtually impossible to reconstruct the social order without first the blessing of God, second the cooperation between men of good will and between nations, and third the reform of moral behavior in society. This will move men from simply seeking their own selfish interests to seeking the common good. Toward the Letter's end Pius gives his own critique of the evils inherent in Socialism and Communism, as well as unrestricted Capitalism and their separate effects on society and on the transcendent human dignity of man. He maintains that Socialism has sunk into Communism with the rise of the Soviet Union, and unregulated Capitalism has been a major contributor to the increasing numbers of both the working and destitute poor in much of the undeveloped world. Pius XI will try to navigate a middle path between collectivist Socialism and unrestricted Capitalism. He sees the only solutions to healing these social wounds to be a "return to Christian life and institutions (QA #129)" and "a return openly and sincerely to the teaching of the Gospel (QA #136)."[3]

This Letter can be found in its entirety at the Vatican Website: http://w2.vatican.va/content/pius-xi/en.html

*Vatican Archives, On the Fortieth Year- (*Quadragesimo Anno*), Pius XI, 1931 http://w2.vatican.va/content/pius-xi/en/encyclicals/documents/hf_p-xi_enc_19310515_quadragesimo-anno.html

Chapter Eleven

Social Letters of Pope John XXIII

MOTHER AND TEACHER-(*MATER ET MAGISTRA),* 1961

Pope John XXIII wrote "Mother and Teacher," (*Mater et Magistra*) in 1961 in celebration of the 70th anniversary of *Rerum Novarum.* To John XXIII, "Mother and Teacher," was the most fitting description he could give to the Catholic Church.[1] Since the last social Encyclical, World War II had come and gone and the threat of world domination by the Third Reich was no longer a factor. The first nuclear bomb was used and caused devastation in Japan. There was an uneasy peace among many of the world's nations and the war did have its economic impact, particularly on many of the poorer persons in society. The worldwide gap between rich and poor had widened.

John begins the Letter by trying to make an immediate connection between the temporal and the eternal regarding the ongoing role of the Catholic Church. After heaping much praise on Pope Leo's writing of *Rerum Novarum*[2] and Pius' subsequent Letter,[3] he begins to outline many of the parts of their Letters he wishes to repeat and affirm. He will use the word, 'Solidarity,' in its literal sense to describe Christian brotherhood for the first time in any papal Letter. Although previous Letters may have tried to describe this solidarity, the word had not been used so commonly in this sense up until now (MM#23, 146, 155-157, 190).[4]

He does credit Pius XI for his formative thoughts on the Principle of Subsidiarity, but makes clear that subsidiarity should be the norm of social policy. There is much more of an expansion of CST on the Principle of Subsidiarity as a necessity in this Letter (MM#117, 152).[5] This is raised because of Marxism, which he declares as "contrary to Christian teaching and the nature of man." It has brought state intervention to a new level (MM#

23).[6] Marxism, on the other hand, will maintain that "religion is the opiate of the people."[7]

He then begins to draw some distinctions that have arisen in society over the past twenty years that make the Principle of Subsidiarity even more important and relevant for its functionality. He writes: "In the twenty years which have elapsed since the changing economic climate noted at that time by Pius XII, the economic scene has undergone a radical transformation, both in the internal structure of the various states and in their relations with one another (MM#46)."

He saw these changes happening principally in the areas of economics, science, and technology. For example, nuclear energy has now entered the mix changing the horrors of warfare. There also have been vast increases in the speed of communications and the invention of the radio and TV. Automation had arrived and there is faster transportation and even the conquest of space. In politics, there is a moving away from colonialism and more independence, especially for countries in Asia and Africa. He is disturbed, however, by the diminishing of freedoms and personal initiative as he sees several states interfering with the delicate balance maintained by subsidiarity through growing state intervention (MM#117).

In the social field, there is the advent of social security systems and the breaking down of class barriers. A few things that disturb him greatly, however, are the widespread disrespect for human dignity and the widening disparity in the distribution of wealth, not only between persons, but countries as well (MM# 48).[8] There are references to a disregard for distributive justice in society in no less than seven sections of the Letter (MM#48, 74, 82-83, 113-115, 136, 168).[9]

Toward the end of the Letter, Pope John will state what he calls "the fundamental principle." That is to establish in no uncertain terms, "of no doubt," that the church's social teaching views "the individual human being as the foundation, cause, and end of every social institution… the church constructs her social teaching around this (MM#218-220)." On the other hand, he will also make clear: "It is not enough merely to formulate a social doctrine. It must be translated into reality. This is particularly true of the Church's social doctrine, the light of which is Truth, Justice its objective, and Love its driving force (MM#226)."[10]

This Letter can be found in its entirety at the Vatican Websitehttp://w2.vatican.va/content/johnxxiii/en.html

PEACE ON EARTH-(*PACEM IN TERRIS*), 1963

As a further step toward truly becoming the "Church in the Modern World," this Letter is addressed to "all men of good will" and not just specifically to Catholics or even simply to Christians.[11]

In 1963, the dangers of a nuclear war were heightened following the construction of the Berlin Wall and the Cuban missile crisis. In America, race relations were tense and racism was rampant, particularly across the South. Pope John's Letter outlines the rights, duties, and responsibilities of people in society to be peacekeepers and maintain good race relations while condemning both nuclear war and racism as two social evils. He recommends: following God's divine order, disarmament, negotiation, agreement, respect for human rights, solidarity, and genuine peace through love of neighbor as some paths to follow. Peace in the world must begin with recognizing the basic human dignity of each human being as being created in the image of God.

He also recommends the Principle of Subsidiarity as a solution to the many "social, political and cultural problems which affect the universal common good (PT #140-141)."[12] He outlines a list of human rights from the outset (PT #11-27). They include the right to life (PT#11), to moral and cultural values (PT #12-13), to worship according to conscience (PT # 14), to freely choose one's state in life (PT #15-17), to have economic rights (PT #18-22), to meeting and association (PT# 23-24), to emigrate and immigrate (PT# 25), and to possess political rights (PT #26-27).[13] These rights are followed by a series of duties and responsibilities necessary to maintain peace, order, and tranquility in society (PT # 28-34).[14] He then reaches the conclusion that before any society can be consonant with human dignity it must be "based on truth…, guided by justice…, and animated by love and freedom (PT # 35-36)."[15]

In addition to seeking a path to peace for both nuclear war and race relations, the Letter will impact CST in areas like church-state relations, religious freedom, women's rights, globalization, rights of developing nations, and international relations. Further, the Letter will also have a tremendous impact on the writing of documents that will present themselves at Vatican Council II which is about two years away. It will greatly impact both the "Pastoral Constitution on the Church in the Modern World" (*Gaudium et Spes)* and "The Declaration on Religious Freedom" (*Dignitatus Humanae*).[16]

In this Letter, Pope John discusses "distributive justice," in his own language without specifically using those two words. He uses different language to discuss a sharing of the world's goods. I will discuss this in detail in Section III of this book.[17]

Peace on Earth, *Pacem in Terris,* became the first piece of CST which was published in its entirety in *The New York Times*.[18] In 1962, John XXIII was diagnosed with cancer and was dying. This Letter was described as his last will and testament and his gift of peace to a troubled world. It was published on April, 11, 1963, just a few weeks before his death.

This Letter can be found in its entirety at the Vatican Website: http://w2.vatican.va/content/john-xxiii/en.html

Chapter Twelve

Social Letters of Vatican Council II, 1965

DOCUMENT ON RELIGIOUS FREEDOM-HUMAN DIGNITY-*DIGNITATIS HUMANAE*

Previous church councils had been convened primarily to combat heresies or to clarify doctrinal issues. Vatican II was different. When John XXIII opened the council, it was declared that its purpose was to "promote peace" and "the unity of all mankind." He would open this, the 21st Council, and Pope Paul VI would close it. It would be the first truly ecumenical council. It would be the climactic decisive move in the Catholic Church truly becoming, "the Church in the Modern World."[1]

Among the more prominent theologians present were Karl Rahner, Yves Congar, Henry Delubac, Hans Kung, Edward Schillebeeckx, and one who would have tremendous influence in the writing of the Document on Religious Freedom, *Dignitatis Humanae*, American Jesuit, John Courtney Murray. Murray's writings (ex. his book, *We Hold These Truths*) were principally a Catholic theology of religious freedom.[2]

Murray, being an American Jesuit, saw no future problems in the United States with the separation of church and state as the Bill of Rights prevented that. This existed as a potential European problem. The problem he foresaw in America was creeping secularism, so he sought a government limited by law to protect and defend all religious communities working in faith together. He had already developed much of his theology by writing many articles for *America Magazine*, the Jesuit monthly publication.

There were four basic truths which Murray wanted to see incorporated into The Document on Religious Freedom, they included:

1. The dignity of the human being.
2. The human person's endowment with natural rights and duties.
3. The juridical nature of the state.
4. The limitations of government powers.

This new document on CST was considered by many to be the most controversial one to come out of Vatican II. Several prior Papal Letters had condemned many facets of religious freedom (ex. Pope Pius IX, *Syllabus of Errors*).[3] There was tremendous pressure from some quarters of the Curia to silence Murray and scrap the document, but with the support of his Jesuit superiors, Cardinal Spellman from New York, and a few other council members, Murray prevailed. The church was now about to make a 180 degree turn from the past in endorsing the Document on Religious Freedom.

Unlike most Letters to come out of Vatican II, this one was very brief. There are only 15 sections contained within the document. Religious freedom is established as being grounded in the human dignity of man who is made in the image of God and man's human dignity is discussed in the first 12 sections of the document in ten separate ways. Rights and duties are also discussed 12 times in the first 14 sections. For example:

"The council further declares that the right to religious freedom has its foundation in the very dignity of the human person, as this dignity is known through the revealed word of God and by reason itself. This right of the human person to religious freedom is to be recognized in the constitutional law whereby society is governed and thus it is to become a civil right (DH #2)."

The role of government to foster, preserve, and protect man's religious freedom is threaded throughout all 15 sections of the Letter. For example:

> Government is also to help create conditions favorable to the fostering of religious life, in order that the people may be truly enabled to exercise their religious rights and to fulfill their religious duties, and in order that society itself may profit by the moral qualities of justice and peace which have their origin in men's faithfulness to God and to His holy will (DH # 6).

To leave no doubt in any reader's mind that the subject matter in *Dignitatis Humanae* concerns the religious freedom of the human person in society protected by government, the words "religious freedom" are used together along with the word, "government," twenty-three times in these short 15 sections. For example:

"Consequently, in order that relationships of peace and harmony be established and maintained within the whole of mankind, it is necessary that religious freedom be everywhere provided with an effective constitutional guarantee and that respect be shown for the high duty and right of man freely to lead his religious life in society (DH #15)."

The two primary directions of the focus on religious freedom in this letter took the tack of treating "religious freedom from" and "religious freedom for." The former describes how human persons, with their inherent human dignity, are transcendent and made in the image of God; therefore, they must be free from coercion all times and under all circumstances. This is particularly from coercion by the state to go against one's conscience (DH # 12). The latter declares that we should possess our religious freedom for exercising reason so that we might seek and act in accordance with the truth, especially that truth which is found in God (DH #11-13).

This Document can be found in its entirety at the Vatican Website: http://w2.vatican.va/archive/hist_councils/ii_vatican_council/documents/vat-ii_decl_19651207_dignitatis-humanae_en.html[4]

PASTORAL CONSTITUTION ON THE CHURCH IN THE MODERN WORLD-*GAUDIUM ET SPES*

Joys and Hopes; *Gaudium et Spes,* is an overview of the Catholic Church's teaching on the human person's relationship to society. It interrelates social justice, economics, culture, poverty, ecumenism, and advances in science, technology, and communications, with the Church's salvific role. Unlike the *Document on Religious Freedom* which is a relatively short letter, *The Pastoral Constitution on the Church* is one of the longest to come out of the Council.

Like turning the altar around to revise the liturgy which occurred at Vatican II, this Letter, in its introductory statement, begins by turning its attention away from the church to look at what is currently going on with the situation of mankind in the modern world.[5] What is first seen is a cultural and social transformation which has a direct bearing on man's religious life. Also seen in the world is a tremendous abundance of wealth, resources and economic power. But, over against that, many of the world's citizens, are living in destitute poverty and hunger. There is certainly seen to be an imbalance in the world, not only in this regard, but an even more basic imbalance which is rooted in men's hearts. The world and society are changing, but the Church maintains that beneath all changes there are many realities which do not change and which have their ultimate foundation in Christ. In this light, the Church declares that she wishes only "to speak to all men in order to shed light on the mystery of man and to cooperate in finding the solution to the outstanding problems of our time… to foresee the problems to come upon us, we should "read the signs of the times." (GS #1-10)

Following this introductory statement, the document, like many others before it since 1891, spends a considerable amount of time addressing the basic human dignity of man, but, concludes that 'The root reason for human dignity lies in man's call to communion with God." It is further concluded, however, that much of the world does not recognize this, has rejected God, and fallen into atheism. "Thus, atheism must be accounted among the most serious problems of this age, and is deserving of closer examination." The church does see a remedy for this; that being: "a proper presentation of the Church's teaching as well as in the integral life of the Church and her members (GS #19-21)."

The Letter then treats the social nature of the human person and how this makes it evident that the progress of the human person and the advance of society hinge on one another. There is an interdependence which is required, and neighbor must be considered another self. Because of the inherent and transcendent dignity of the human person, the social order and its development must invariably work to the benefit of each and all human persons. Therefore, this social order must be "founded on truth, built on justice and animated by love; in freedom, it should grow every day toward a more humane balance." There is a "solidarity" required to achieve social and economic goals which must be constantly increased until that day on which it will be brought to perfection in Christ (GS #26-32).

A discussion follows on the individual and collective activities of man through the ages and the purposes of these activities. There is seen to be a need for a closer bond between these activities and the Christian religion. Then the *Pastoral Constitution on the Church* begins to approach what I believe is the real social message of this Letter and that is "The Role of the Church in the Modern World." The Catholic Church would no longer be a church of triumphalism or assimilation or a medieval institution. She would be a church who as part of her salvific role, would listen to society and then express her pastoral mission often in socio-economic terms. This reality was evolving as a part of a growing body of Catholic thought called CST, and it was occurring much to the chagrin of many in the church who wanted the church to speak only in fully divine terms about heaven and not fully human terms about earth.

This role is seen to be twofold: both a saving role and an eschatological or end- times role. She is to facilitate in bringing about the goal of man which is to reveal the mystery of God while continuing to uncover the meaning of man's own existence. There is an evolution toward unity happening in the world as a process of "socialization and association" in civic and economic realms. Although the Church does not see herself as having any proper specified mission in the political, economic or social order and her purpose is seen to be a religious one; she is a universal church, and out of this religious mission can come a consolidation of the human community according to the divine law.

Thus, because mankind has transcendent human dignity, there is always another "Tale of Two Cities," going on. Mankind should see itself as working out our salvation both in the 'earthly city,' and in the 'heavenly city.' Lay people will be asked to take a greater role in all of this, and their role would be expanded upon in a separate Document of the council, *The Document on the Laity.*[6]

It is in the world's interest to acknowledge the Church as an historical reality and to recognize her good influence in her role. The Church herself should know how richly she has profited by the history and social/spiritual development of humanity and the dignity of man's existence. While helping the world and receiving many benefits from it, the Church ultimately has a single intentional role: that "God's kingdom may come, and that the salvation of the whole human race may come to pass…the Church in the Modern World must fulfill her role as 'the universal sacrament of salvation' (GS # 40-45)."

Finally, there are seen to be some problems of special urgency which must be discussed. They pertain to marriage and the family, human progress, life in its economic, social and political dimensions, the bonds between the family of nations, and peace. Therefore, the church, in her role, can first offer guidance and support to those who are trying to preserve the holiness, to foster the natural dignity of the married state, and proclaim and defend marriage and family life with its superlative value. The church can also assist in the proper development of human culture by always reminding society that human culture should be subordinated to the integral perfection of the human person, to the good of the community and of the whole society. It will always seek to harmonize human culture with Christian culture whenever possible.

Regarding distributive justice, the Letter does address economic development. The church believes that it must remain under man's determination. It should not be left to the judgment of a few men or groups possessing too much economic power or the political community alone or certain more powerful nations.

In politics, the church believes that it needs to reprove those political systems prevailing in some parts of the world which hamper civic or religious freedom. She advocates: "the establishing of political life on a truly human basis than by fostering an inward sense of justice and kindliness, and of service to the common good (GS #73)." However, she does not see her role as being carried out so much in the political realm:

> The Church, in her role and competence, is not identified in any way with the political community nor bound to any political system. She is at once a sign and a safeguard of the transcendent character of the human person (GS #76).

The Letter closes with a plea for peace in a troubled world. The Principle of Subsidiarity is stressed as being important in regulating economic relations. But here the church, in her role, must also remind the world that there can be no peace without justice. No peace, no justice; no justice, no peace:

> It is likewise this community's duty, with due regard for the Principle of Subsidiarity, so to regulate economic relations throughout the world that these will be carried out in accordance with the norms of justice (GS #86).

And:

> Peace is not merely the absence of war; nor can it be reduced solely to the maintenance of a balance of power between enemies; nor is it brought about by dictatorship. Instead, it is rightly and appropriately called an enterprise of justice...peace is likewise the fruit of love, which goes beyond what justice can provide (GS #78).

Peace between nations can certainly happen and the church can play her role in it by continually pointing the way to "The Prince of Peace (GS #78)." But peace must begin with peace in our hearts first and genuine love for one another. The Letter closes with a quote from John's Gospel: "By this will all men know that you are my disciples, if you have love for one another (John 13:35) (GS #93)."

This Document can be found in its entirety at the Vatican Website: http://www.vatican.va/archive/hist_councils/ii_vatican_council/documents/vat-ii_cons_19651207_gaudium-et-spes_en.html[7]

Chapter Thirteen

Social Letters of Pope Paul VI

THE PROGRESS OF PEOPLES-*POPULORUM PROGRESSIO,* 1967

Although Pope Paul VI wrote seven Papal Encyclicals, this was his first social Letter written during his papacy. This Letter concerns just what the name indicates. It pertains to the progressive development of peoples, and it points out-particularly those who are trying to escape the ravages of hunger, poverty, disease and ignorance. It also highlights those who are seeking a larger share in the benefits of civilization, a more active improvement of their human qualities, and those who consciously strive for fuller growth. Paul VI goes on to praise much in the way of previous CST contained in Letters we've just discussed, such as *On the* New *Things, The Fortieth Year, Mother and Teacher, and Peace on Earth.* [1]

Because of his extensive travels, Paul had witnessed first- hand, the poverty and hunger now spread over much of the globe. He was the first Pope to travel world-wide and thus was writing this Letter from the heart. The Letter points out that in the progress of peoples and their development, an unbridled liberalism has given birth to a type of unrestrained Capitalism which has then given rise to hardships and unjust practices. Its concepts present profit as the chief spur to economic progress, free competition as the guiding norm of economics, and private ownership of the means of production as an absolute right. It sets no limits or sees itself as having any social obligations. To correct this imbalance and injustice, rich nations must contribute to the development of poorer nations. Reforms are necessary.

A new 'solidarity' amongst the brotherhood of man in the world is required. Social justice and universal charity will help to rectify this situation. It is a matter of utmost urgency, however, and world civilization depends on it. (PP #17, 44, 48, 52, 62-73, 84) A 'Justice and Peace Commission' will be established to facilitate this (PP #5).

This Letter can be found in its entirety at the Vatican Website: http://w2.vatican.va/content/paul-vi/en.html[2]

ON THE EIGHTIETH YEAR-*OCTOGESIMA ADVENIENS,* 1971

This Letter was written to Cardinal Maurice Roy, President of the Council on the Laity and the Justice and Peace Commission. It was written in celebration of the 80th year of *Rerum Novarum*[3] "to inspire action for social justice …in response to the new needs of a changing world (OA #1)."

This Letter will come very close to using the terminology 'preferential option for the poor' when referring to the poor of the world in this manner: "In teaching us charity, the Gospel instructs us in the preferential respect due to the poor (OA #23)."

There are also new social problems which have arisen. Urbanization, for example, has necessitated many people with miserable economic situations to begin moving off the land into the cities without any jobs. Also, countless new cases of professional and regional unemployment, as well as unlimited competition utilizing the modern means of publicity is incessantly launching new products to attract the consumer. Superfluous needs are being created and man may be becoming the slave of the objects he makes. This problem is the beginning of what would later be called 'Consumerism' or 'Conspicuous Consumption.' There are additional widespread problems among youth, women, and workers as well as the exploitation of nature and an all-out attack on the environment which could possibly destroy it. Discrimination, particularly in America, as well as the growth of false ideologies is also complicating mankind's existence in society (OA # 8-21).

The Church is doing all it can to bring Christians face to face with these many new problems which have arisen. It is with all the dynamism of CST that the Church accompanies men in their search (OA #42), "But, Christians need to be awakened… and called to action… Structures need to be changed (OA #45)." There is also a need for greater 'solidarity' among the 'universal brotherhood of man' called for in many parts of the Letter to meet the problems and accomplish the tasks at hand in the world (OA #5, 12, 17-18, 23, 31, 41-50). Individual local churches should respond to unjust situations particularly, and act for justice locally. Christians should also think about political solutions even though all of the solutions won't be found there and laity must seek to "renew the temporal order (OA # 46-48)."

This Letter can be found in its entirety at the Vatican Website: http://w2.vatican.va/content/paul-vi/en.html[4]

Chapter Fourteen

Social Letters of John Paul II, 1981-1987

THROUGH WORK-*LABOREM EXERCENS,* 1981

The Letter, written on the 90th anniversary of *Rerum Novarum,*[1] begins with a blessing and then an immediate call to work. Work had changed dramatically since the Industrial Revolution. In a similar fashion to previous CST Letters, there are seen to be many new developments in the world that will affect technological, economic and political conditions which will influence the world of work. All these will require a reordering and re-adjustment of the structures of the modern economy and of the distribution of work.

John Paul doesn't start by 'reading the signs of the times.' He appears to be looking at work somewhat differently than in previous CST Letters. He doesn't seem to want to attempt to change society as much as to place work in its proper context, and to look at the body of theology contained in CST in the light of the concept of human work as a dimension of all that is human.

Citing several earlier papal social Letters, the question of distributive justice and its relation to work is addressed several times in sections 2 through 20. A few examples are:

> The disproportionate distribution of wealth and poverty and the existence of some countries and continents that are developed and of others that are not call for a levelling out and for a search for ways to ensure just development for all (LE #2).

And:

> Here we return once more to the first principle of the whole ethical and social order, namely, the principle of the common use of goods. In every system, regardless of the fundamental relationships within it between capital and labor,

> wages, that is to say remuneration for work, are still a practical means whereby most people can have access to those goods which are intended for common use: both the goods of nature and manufactured goods (LE #19).

Work is a 'key' which is at the center of the social question and now it is more than a class question; it is a world question. The Church sees her role to always call attention to the dignity and rights of those who work, to condemn situations in which that dignity and those rights are violated, and to help to guide the above-mentioned changes to ensure authentic progress by man and society (LE #1-3).

There is an unfolding of the historical-critical understanding of work in the Bible and in the ancient world beginning with the book of Genesis, the conclusion of which seems to be that 'man was not made for work; work was made for man' (LE #4-7). There is also a call for 'worker solidarity,' workers' rights (including the disabled), and ownership which is threaded throughout the Letter stressing the importance of wages, social benefits and unions (LE #8-20).

Perhaps, one of the things going on in John Paul's mind as he writes this Letter on work, is the establishment of the independent, but Catholic based, trade union called 'Solidarity' in his native Poland the year prior in 1980. Poland had been immersed in Marxist/Communist/Socialist/Capitalist struggles and there were socio-economic consequences that gave rise to the worker's longing for justice, freedom, and human dignity which were contained in the Solidarity movement.[2]

He stresses that the Church does see a role for the state in the economy different from that proposed by both American conservatives and American liberals. The state is not to be just a sheriff who benevolently maintains law and order, and because of the Principle of Subsidiarity should the state become directly involved in solving every problem. Instead, as the safeguard of the common good, she must be concerned with the entire life of her citizens and direct, supervise, encourage, restrain, and coordinate the efforts of other groups. These groups will directly address the various problems that arise in the social order (LE #8).

In discussing labor, capital, and property ownership in the Letter, John Paul will prioritize labor stating that it takes precedence over capital. Labor should and must have a focus on the laborer and not on the tasks of the labor or the capital being produced by the labor. As his predecessors had in their Letters, he will also reinforce once again the core message of CST which is "people before things." Of course, when one considers work apart from man, who is a person with transcendent human dignity, only then will work be viewed as a thing (LE # 11-23).

In the last part of *Laborem Exercens*, John Paul outlines what could be called either a "spirituality of work, a Gospel of work, or even perhaps the

Christian understanding of work," because of the life, death, and resurrection of Jesus Christ (LE #24-27). The conclusion seems to be that all work, though it is human, is dignified and divinized because it is a sharing in God's work. This would render all human work, in the end, to be ultimately more important than any economic products or services that would be created by it.

This Letter can be found in its entirety at the Vatican Website: http://w2.vatican.va/content/john-paul-ii/en.html[3]

THE SOCIAL CONCERN OF THE CHURCH-
SOLLICITUDO REI SOCIALIS, 1987

From the opening sentence of the Letter, John Paul II establishes that it will address "the social concern of the Church," directed towards an authentic development of man and society which would respect and promote all the dimensions of the human person." So, it will focus on the interrelation of the social concern of the church, the development of man and society, and the human dignity of man (SS#1).

He begins by discussing the enduring relevance, breadth of outlook, novel character, and originality of his predecessor Paul VI's Letter, *On the Progress of Peoples*[4] , and the rich teaching contained in it. It was now the 20th anniversary of that Letter. He will pay homage and then reaffirm and renew the continuity of CST. He sees this as being both "unchanging" because it is linked with the Gospel, as well as "ever new" because of the continual changes in the life of people and society.

As John Paul begins to survey the contemporary world, he sees that there are some changes since the time of Paul VI's Letter. For one, the hopes for development which existed at that time have not been realized in the twenty years that have passed. Further the situation among the poor of the world has worsened as there are today many millions more in poverty, particularly in underdeveloped countries. This Letter will further develop the concept of "Preferential Option for the Poor" as an important facet of CST.[5] The Pope also attempts perhaps, to present one of the positive arguments contained in Liberation Theology. The *Social Concern of the Church* will take its shape in many directions. It will be a theological, philosophical, political, social, economic, and pastoral letter.

The gap has widened between the developed North and the developing South. The gap in the cultural level between North and South has also widened considerably more and is equally as disturbing. The interdependence of peoples which could bring them closer and is so necessary for authentic development seems like it has stretched further. Finally, if "development is the new name for peace" as Paul's Letter stated, then instead of being on the brink of peace, the nations of the world are closer to the brink of war. The advances in atomic weapons over the past twenty years, now makes possible total and complete annihilation of the planet. The real tragedy is that the money spent to fuel the arms race could have been spent to alleviate people's poverty and suffering. (SS #11-26)

Authentic human development, because the word "development" itself is linked to an economic concept, is in crisis mode. Unless all the resources and potential at man's disposal are guided by a moral understanding and by an orientation towards the true good of humanity, it easily turns against man to oppress him. Many have become slaves of their possessions in a civilization of "consumerism" or (conspicuous) "consumption." No thought is given that some human person somewhere on the planet may be poorer because of it. John Paul reaches a few conclusions regarding this: First, that for those who believe in the Word of God, today's "development" is to be seen as a moment in the story which began at creation- a story which is constantly endangered by reason of infidelity to the Creator's will, and especially by the temptation to idolatry. Also, development which does not respect and promote human rights—personal and social, economic and political, including the rights of nations and of peoples- cannot be worthy of man.

Progress is not development and the "structures of sin" are obstacles. Finally, what must be recognized is each person's equal right "to be seated at the table of the common banquet," instead of lying outside the door like Lazarus, while "the dogs come and lick his sores" (cf. Lk 16:21).[6] To be authentic, development must be achieved within the framework of solidarity and freedom (SS # 27-34).

John Paul then attempts to discuss authentic human development not just as a socio-economic term, but as a theological term because of its moral relevance. He concludes this theological argument by stating:

> The Church's social doctrine is not a 'third way' between liberal capitalism and Marxist collectivism . . . rather, it constitutes a category of its own. Nor is it an ideology, but rather the accurate formulation of the results of a careful reflection on the complex realities of human existence, in society and in the international order, in the light of faith and of the Church's tradition . . . its aim is thus to guide Christian behavior. It therefore belongs to the field, not of ideology, but of theology and particularly of moral theology (SS# 41).

In this Letter, John Paul will not align himself with the thinking of the Capitalist West or the Totalitarian East. He sees them as both being responsible for the poor and suffering in the world, but for different reasons. He presents theological arguments which he believes transcend any geo-politics. This was a late decision on the part of John Paul II. He had thought about an approach which showed a distinction between the Capitalist West and the Totalitarian East, in that the Capitalist system was at least capable of self-correction. He decided against this approach to be more even-handed. He attempted to try to stay above the fray with theological arguments offering love of neighbor, freedom, rejecting the structures of sin, and solidarity as possible solutions. At this moment in time, this could only be potentially acceptable to the West anyway.

Regarding distributive justice, there is much said about it as economic injustice in the Letter which will be discussed later in the final section of this book.

In the Letter's last section, John Paul outlines his conclusions:

> Development which is merely economic is incapable of setting man free, on the contrary, it will end by enslaving him further . . . At stake is the dignity of the human person, whose defense and promotion have been entrusted to us by the Creator . . . Christians and others of good will should . . . implement—by the way they live as individuals and as families, by the use of their resources, by their civic activity, by contributing to economic and political decisions and by personal commitment to national and international undertakings—the measures inspired by solidarity and love of preference for the poor . . . It is appropriate to emphasize the preeminent role that belongs to the laity, both men and women . . . It is their task to animate temporal realities with Christian commitment, by which they show that they are witnesses and agents of peace and justice . . . By sharing the good you give us, may we secure justice and equality for every human being, an end to all division and a human society built on love and peace. This, in conclusion, is what I ask in the name of all my brothers and sisters, to whom I send a special blessing as a sign of greeting and good wishes (SS #46-49).

This Letter can be found in its entirety at the Vatican Website: http://w2.vatican.va/content/john-paul-ii/en.html[7]

Chapter Fifteen

Social Letters of John Paul II, 1991-1995

THE ONE HUNDREDTH YEAR-*CENTESSIMUS ANNUS,* 1991

As the title of John Paul II's social Letter indicates, The One Hundredth Year-*Centessimus Annus,* it has now been one hundred years since the writing of that foundational Letter of CST, On the New Things-*Rerum Novarum.*[1] From the outset, he calls his predecessor's Letter an "immortal document" and uses it as "an invitation to look around at the "new things" which surround us . . . and he uses that Letter to "look to the future" as well. (CA # 1-4)

After discussing what "new things" were going on in the world at the time of the writing of *Rerum Novarum*, he then begins to discuss many events in the world since to focus on the "new things" going on in the world now as he writes this anniversary Letter (CA # 5-11). First, there are negative consequences which Pope Leo foresaw— political, social and economic — of the social order proposed by "Socialism." It had appeared on the world scene promising to reverse the positions of the poor and the rich, but ended up being increasingly detrimental to the very people whom it was meant to help. The good of the individual ended up being completely subordinated to the functioning of the socio-economic mechanism. Instead of "Utopian Socialism," he will label this as "Real Socialism" (CA # 12-16).

It seems that the whole concept of freedom in the current day has become distorted. It has now become detached from truth and the duty to respect other's rights, having fallen into self-love with contempt for God and neighbor. Self-love has become self-interest, refusing to be limited by any demand of justice (CA # 17).

There exists a situation of non-war among powerful nations, but unfortunately non-war is not peace. In fact, the precariousness of the peace which followed the Second World War was one of the principal causes of the militarization of many Third World countries. Money is being spent all over the world on arms, to the detriment of meeting the needs of many poor and hungry people. Another kind of response is represented by the affluent society or the consumer society. It seeks to show how a free-market society can achieve a greater satisfaction of material human needs than Communism, while equally excluding spiritual values. It denies an autonomous existence and value to morality, law, culture and religion. This model has ended up agreeing with Marxism in the sense that it totally reduces man to the sphere of economics and the satisfaction of material needs. Wealth and power are in the hands of the few, and there is no distributive justice (CA # 17-20).

As John Paul discusses the year 1989, he sees the fall of Marxism having a great impact on the division of the planet into worlds which are closed to one another and in jealous competition. This has further highlighted the reality of the need for interdependence among peoples. Particularly, Third World countries are in desperate need of assistance due to situations of extreme poverty and want. Development must not be regarded as strictly an economic term, but a way that is fully human. He sees the apex of development to be the right and duty to seek God, to know him and to live in accordance with that knowledge (CA # 22-29).

There is much said by the Holy Father concerning distributive justice in this Letter which will be discussed in the final section of this book. The Letter also expresses some concern about the ecological question and destruction of the environment. John Paul relates this to the problem of consumerism and sees a close connection.

He clearly states that the Marxist system has failed and goes on to discuss some positives and negatives inherent in the Capitalist systems, but the spread of atheism can be attributed to both systems. He also says that the church has no models of her own to present; however, he encourages the principles of subsidiarity, solidarity, and social justice in all current economic models (CA #30-43).

Rerum Novarum had stated that society needs to be organized into three branches, legislative, executive, and judicial and each of these three powers would be kept in balance by the others. This would reflect man's social nature and insure freedoms for all. It would be the "Rule of Law" and it would be sovereign. Totalitarianism not only rejected the "Rule of Law," but rejected the church as well. Further, it absorbed within itself the nation, society, the family, religious groups, and individuals themselves. Following the collapse of Communist totalitarianism, we are witnessing a domination of the democratic ideal together with a concern for human rights. But, even in countries with democratic forms of government, these rights are not always fully respected. The scandal of abortion is given as an example, and certain other decisions are being made without regard to justice or morality.

Regarding the state, he calls upon it to be the agent of justice for the poor. There seems to be generally more intervention by the state than necessary. This has led to the creation of a new type of State, the so-called "Welfare State.'" It has probably occurred because the Principle of Subsidiarity has been neglected. The church, like its founder, the Lord Jesus Christ, wishes to align herself on the side of the poor and needy. It is in solidarity with them as well as with families and other intermediate communities.

All human activity takes place within a culture and interacts with culture. The involvement of the whole man is required, whereby he exercises his creativity, intelligence, and knowledge of the world and of people. Furthermore, he displays his capacity for self-control, personal sacrifice, solidarity, and readiness to promote the common good. The way in which he is involved in building his own future depends on the understanding he has of himself and of his own destiny. It is on this level that the Church's specific and decisive contribution to true culture is to be found.

Due to the war between nations, and with the Persian Gulf War in mind, John Paul echoes Paul VI and repeats the refrain "development is the new name for peace" (CA # 44-52). In the final section of the letter, Pope John Paul concludes by discussing how "Man is the Way of the Church." Through the incarnation and the mystery of Christ, God has united Godself with each man forever. Today the church's social doctrine focuses on the human dignity of man and the complex network of relationships man has in society. Therefore, CST begins in faith and by its concern for man and the way he conducts himself in society. This "Christian anthropology" properly belongs to the field of theology and particularly of moral theology. As far as the Church is concerned, the social message of the Gospel found in CST must not be considered a theory, but above all else, as a basis and motivation for action. Love for others, and in the first place a preferential love for the poor, in whom the Church sees Christ himself, is made concrete in the promotion of justice.

This will require above all a change of life-styles, of models of production and consumption, and of the established structures of power. Therefore, in order that the demands of justice may be met, what is needed is the gift of grace, a gift which comes from God.

Dialogue and cooperation is required of all people of good will, particularly individuals and groups with specific responsibilities in the areas of politics, economics and social life, at both the national and international levels. In the world, some have much and others have nothing. The church will continue to call this unjust. The church's position will always align her with the dignity of man and particularly with the poor and vulnerable in society. This call she knows will not win the favor of the church with everyone (CA # 53-62).

This Letter can be found in its entirety at the Vatican Website: http://w2.vatican.va/content/john-paul-ii/en.html[2]

THE GOSPEL OF LIFE-*EVANGELIUM VITAE,* 1995

John Paul's final social Letter begins by stating that "The Gospel of Life is at the heart of Jesus message." It goes on to stress the dignity of each human life as being of "inestimable value" as it is a "sharing in the very life of God," and it will "reach its full realization in eternity (EV # 1-2)." Today there exists, new threats to human life especially where "life is weak and defenseless . . . " These are infamies and opposed to life, they include: any type of murder, genocide, abortion, euthanasia, as well as self-destruction. They also include whatever violates the integrity of the human person, such as mutilation, torments inflicted on body or mind, attempts to coerce the will, subhuman living conditions, arbitrary imprisonment, deportation, slavery, prostitution, human trafficking, disgraceful working conditions, and treating people as mere instruments of gain rather than as free and responsible persons. Many of these are now justified by so-called "rights of individual freedom." The result of this is tragic: not only in destruction of lives, but conscience itself, darkened as it were, by such widespread conditioning, is finding it increasingly difficult to distinguish between good and evil in what concerns the basic value of human life. (EV # 3-4)."

The climate of widespread moral uncertainty can, in some way, be explained by the multiplicity and gravity of today's social problems...But, it is no less true that we are confronted by an even larger reality, which can be described as a "veritable structure of sin." This reality is characterized by the emergence of a culture which denies solidarity and in many cases, takes the form of a veritable "culture of death." In this way, a kind of "conspiracy against life" is unleashed. To facilitate the spread of abortion, enormous sums of money have been invested and continue to be invested in the production of pharmaceutical products which make it possible to kill the fetus in the mother's womb without recourse to medical assistance. Further, it is frequently asserted that contraception, if made safe and available to all, is the most effective remedy against abortion. The Catholic Church is then accused of promoting abortion, because she obstinately continues to teach the moral unlawfulness of contraception (EV #12-13).

> There also exists in contemporary culture a certain 'Promethean attitude' which leads people to think that they can control life and death by taking the decisions about them into their own hands . . . In the rich and developed nations, there is a disturbing decline of the birthrate . . . The poorer countries, on the other hand, generally have a high rate of population growth . . . Contraception, sterilization and abortion are certainly part of the reason why in some

> cases there is a sharp decline in the birthrate. It is not difficult to be tempted to use the same methods and attacks against life where there is also a situation of demographic explosion (EV #15-16).
>
> Freedom negates and destroys itself, and becomes a factor leading to the destruction of others, when it no longer recognizes and respects its essential link with the truth . . . To claim the right to abortion, infanticide and euthanasia, and to recognize that right in law, means to attribute to human freedom a perverse and evil significance: that of an absolute power over others and against others . . . When the sense of God is lost, the sense of man is also threatened and poisoned...Man is no longer able to see himself as "mysteriously different" from other earthly creatures . . . he is somehow reduced to being "a thing", and no longer grasps the 'transcendent character of his existence as man' . . . The eclipse of the sense of God and of man inevitably leads to a practical materialism, which breeds individualism, utilitarianism and hedonism . . . The unconditional choice for life reaches its full religious and moral meaning when it flows from, is formed by and nourished by faith in Christ (EV # 19-28).

The struggle between life and death; good and evil, begins and ends with Jesus Christ who came that "we might have life." An entire section of this Letter grounds this "Gospel of Life" in passages from both the Old and New Testaments. For example:

> Hence, with our attention fixed on the Lord Jesus, we wish to hear from him once again 'the words of God' (Jn. 3:34)[3] and meditate anew on the Gospel of life. The deepest and most original meaning of this meditation on what revelation tells us about human life was taken up by the Apostle John in the opening words of his First Letter: 'That which was from the beginning, which we have heard, which we have seen with our eyes, which we have looked upon and touched with our hands, concerning the word of life-the life was made manifest, and we saw it, and testify to it, and proclaim to you the eternal life which was with the Father and was made manifest to us-that which we have seen and heard we proclaim also to you, so that you may have fellowship with us (Jn.1:1-3)[4] (EV # 29-51).
>
> As Christians, we are called to keep God's commandments, but, God's commandments are never detached from his love . . . The Gospel of Life is both a great gift of God and an exacting task for humanity . . . The gift thus becomes a commandment, and the commandment is itself a gift. The precept 'You shall not kill' is strongly negative: it indicates the extreme limit which can never be exceeded. Implicitly however, it encourages a positive attitude of absolute respect for life . . . As far as the right to life is concerned, every innocent human being is equal to all others. This equality is the basis of all authentic social relationships which, to be truly such, can only be founded on truth and justice . . . Among all the crimes which can be committed against life, procured abortion has characteristics making it particularly serious and deplorable . . . At the other end of life's spectrum, men and women find themselves facing the mystery of death . . . In this context the temptation grows to have recourse to euthanasia, that is, to take control of death . . . In

> reality, what might seem logical and humane, when looked at more closely, is seen to be senseless and inhumane . . . Abortion and euthanasia are thus crimes which no human law can claim to legitimize (EV # 52-78).

The final sections of the Letter pertain to the necessity of answering the call to proclaim the Gospel of Life through proclaiming the Gospel of Jesus Christ, the living God who gives life. Doctors, nurses, health care workers, pharmacists, volunteers, chaplains, civil leaders, public officials, and families all bear a greater responsibility for doing this because of their respective roles. The formation of conscience and education play important parts in bringing about a culture of life. There is also contained in this section a special message to women, particularly women who have had an abortion (EV # 79-101).

The conclusion of the Letter turns our attention back to the one whose "yes" answered the call of the Gospel of Life; Mary, the mother of the Lord Jesus Christ and our mother. There remains the mutual relationship between the mystery of the Church and Mary which has given birth to the church's "spiritual motherhood." The final words of the Gospel of Life are contained in a poem dedicated on the Feast of the Annunciation to Mary, mother of the living (EV # 102-105).

This Letter can be found in its entirety at the Vatican Website: http://w2.vatican.va/content/john-paul-ii/en.html[5]

Chapter Sixteen

Social Letter of Pope Benedict XVI, 2009

CHARITY IN TRUTH-*CARITAS IN VERITATE,* 2009

Pope Benedict's Letter, Charity in Truth, begins by first bearing witness to Jesus Christ who "bore witness by his earthly life and especially by his death and resurrection," and who, "is the principal driving force behind the authentic development of every person and of all humanity (CV # 1)."

Charity is at the heart of the Church's social doctrine. However, in society today, charity can be misconstrued. Through its close link with truth, charity can be recognized as an authentic expression of humanity and as an element of fundamental importance in human relations, including those of a public nature. Only in truth does charity shine forth; only in truth can charity be authentically lived. Without truth, charity can become mere sentimentality, and love an empty shell. Jesus is both *Agápe and Lógos*: Charity and Truth, Love and Word. (CV #2-3).

This dynamic of charity received and given is what gives rise to the Church's social teaching, which is *caritas in veritate in re sociali*: the proclamation of the truth of Christ's love in society. Charity goes beyond justice. Love in truth, *Caritas in Veritate*, is a great challenge for the Church in a world that is becoming progressively and pervasively globalized. Fidelity to man requires fidelity to the truth, which alone is the guarantee of freedom (cf. Jn. 8:32)[1] and of the possibility of integral human development (CV # 4-9).

Pope Benedict pays deserved tribute and then gives a review of many of the Letters written by Paul VI, particularly, *Populorem Progressio,*[2] which he singles out because it allows him, some forty years later, to remain faithful to its message of charity and truth. Its perspectives remain fundamental for providing direction to the church's commitment to the development of peoples today. It also underlines the urgent need for reform and sheds light on the great continuing problems of injustice in the development of peoples. The call for courageous action needs to be taken without delay (CV #10-20).

Profit has become an end all, be all. Today, profit is placed before people, and society has lost sight of the common good. Inequalities are on the increase and today there exists a "scandal of inequalities." Benedict then reminds everyone, "especially governments engaged in boosting the world's economic and social assets, that the primary capital to be safeguarded and valued is man, the human person in his or her integrity: Man is the source, the focus and the aim of all economic and social life (CV #21-25)."

Life in many poor countries is still extremely insecure because of food shortages, and feeding the hungry is an ethical imperative for the universal Church. It is therefore necessary to cultivate a public conscience that considers food and access to water as universal rights of all human beings, without distinction or discrimination. Respect for life cannot be detached from questions concerning the development of peoples. Not only does poverty still provoke high rates of infant mortality, but some parts of the world still experience practices of demographic control on the part of governments that often promote contraception and even go so far as to impose abortion.

There is another aspect of modern life that is very closely connected to development: the denial of the right to religious freedom. Furthermore, the dignity of the individual and the demands of justice require, particularly today, that economic choices do not cause disparities in wealth to increase in an excessive and morally unacceptable manner. More than forty years since the writing of *Populorem Progressio*, progress remains an open question. There has been an explosion of worldwide interdependence, commonly known as globalization. Originating within economically developed countries, this process by its nature has spread to include all economies. Without the guidance of charity in truth, this global force could cause unprecedented damage and create new divisions within the human family. Hence, charity and truth confront us with an altogether new and creative challenge to broaden the scope of reason and make it capable of knowing and directing these powerful new forces (CV #26-33).

In Section Three of the Letter there is a very clear call for the increase of distributive justice in society which will be discussed at length in the final section of this book. Section four of the Letter is concerned with the development of people, rights and duties, and the environment. Rights presuppose duties, if they are not to become mere license. An overemphasis on rights leads to a disregard for duties. Duties set a limit on rights because they point to the human and ethical framework of which rights are a part, in this way ensuring that they do not become license.

Duties thereby reinforce rights and call for their defense and promotion…in the service of the common good. Governments can lose sight of the objectivity and inviolability of rights. When this happens, the authentic development of peoples is endangered, so the sharing of reciprocal duties is a more powerful incentive to action than the mere assertion of rights. The notion of rights and duties in development must also take account of the problems associated with population growth, a very important aspect of authentic development, since it concerns the inalienable values of life and the family.

In countries excluded from the influential circles of the global economy, it is very important to move ahead with projects based on subsidiarity, suitably planned and managed, aimed at affirming rights yet also providing for the assumption of corresponding responsibilities.

Today the subject of development is also closely related to the duties arising from our relationship to the natural environment. The environment is God's gift to everyone, and in our use of it we have a responsibility towards the poor, towards future generations, and humanity. It is more than raw material to be manipulated at our pleasure; it is a wondrous work of the Creator; therefore, it must be used wisely and not exploited.

The covenant between human beings and the environment needs to be strengthened and all international leaders should act jointly to show a readiness to work in good faith, respecting the law and promoting solidarity with the weakest regions of the planet. Every violation of solidarity harms the environment; therefore, the way humanity treats the environment will determine how it treats itself and how the environment will treat us. Nature is one and indivisible: it takes in not only the environment but also life, sexuality, marriage, the family, social relations: in a word, integral human development (CV #43-52).

The development of peoples depends, above all, on recognizing that humanity is a single family working together in true communion. All peoples within the one community of the human family should be knit together in solidarity with the fundamental values of justice and peace. As a spiritual being, the human creature is defined through interpersonal relations and one of the deepest forms of poverty a person can experience is isolation.

Cooperation for development must not be concerned exclusively with the economic dimension: it offers a wonderful opportunity for encounter between cultures and peoples. In all cultures, there are examples of ethical convergence, some isolated, some interrelated, as an expression of the one human nature, willed by the Creator; the tradition of ethical wisdom knows this as the natural law. This universal moral law provides a sound basis for all cultural, religious and political dialogue.

In the search for solutions to the current economic crisis, development aid for poor countries must be considered a valid means of creating wealth for all. In the face of the unrelenting growth of global interdependence, there is a strong need for a reform of the United Nations Organization, and likewise of economic institutions and international finance, so that the concept of the family of nations can acquire real teeth. One also senses the urgent need to find innovative ways of implementing the principle of the responsibility to protect and give poorer nations an effective voice in shared decision-making. This seems necessary to arrive at a political, juridical and economic order which can increase and give direction to international cooperation for the development of all peoples in solidarity (CV #53-67).

Next, Benedict will outline many of the dangers of technological progress. The challenge of development today is closely linked to technological progress but, technology is never merely technology. It reveals man and his aspirations toward development; it expresses the inner tension that impels him gradually to overcome material limitations. True development does not consist primarily in "doing." The key to development is a mind capable of thinking in technological terms and grasping the fully human meaning of human activities, within the context of the holistic meaning of the individual's "being." Human freedom is authentic only when it responds to the fascination of technology with decisions that are the fruit of moral responsibility.

Linked to technological development is the increasingly pervasive presence of the means of social communications. It is almost impossible today to imagine the life of the human family without them. Reason and faith can come to each other's assistance. Only together will they save man, as reason without faith is doomed to flounder in an illusion of its own omnipotence. Faith without reason risks being cut off from everyday life.

The social question has become a radically anthropological question, in the sense that it concerns not just how life is conceived but also how it is manipulated. Bio-technology places it increasingly under man's control. In-vitro fertilization, embryo research, the possibility of manufacturing clones and human hybrids: all this is now emerging and being promoted in today's highly disillusioned culture, which believes it has mastered every mystery, because the origin of life is now within our grasp. The "Culture of Death" has powerful new instruments at its disposal such as the scourge of abortion and euthanasia.

There cannot be holistic development and universal common good unless people's spiritual and moral welfare is considered in their totality as body and soul. Knowing is not simply a material act, since the object that is known always conceals something beyond the empirical datum. All our knowledge, even the most simplistic, is always a minor miracle. Mystery is the home of reality. In every truth, there is always something more than we would have expected, in the love that we receive there is always an element that surprises us. It requires new eyes and a new heart, capable of rising above a materialistic vision of human events, capable of glimpsing in development the "beyond" that technology cannot give. By following this path, it is possible to pursue the integral human development that takes its direction from the driving force of charity in truth (CV #68-77).

Pope Benedict concludes his open Letter by asking society to recognize the fact that without God we will never know the way to go. He repeats the words of Jesus who teaches us, "Apart from me you can do nothing" (Jn. 15:5) and then encourages us: "I am with you always, to the close of the age" (Mt. 28:20).[3] He asks us to be aware that the greatest service to development is a Christian humanism that enkindles charity and takes its lead from truth. Furthermore, that rejection of God through atheism makes us oblivious to the Creator and runs the risk of our becoming equally oblivious to human values. This constitutes some of the chief obstacles to development today. Society needs prayer-filled Christians moved by the knowledge that truth-filled love, *caritas in veritate*, from which authentic development proceeds, is not produced by us, but given to us. We should therefore, place our trust in God, who is the beginning and end of all that is good (CV #78-79).

This Letter can be found in its entirety at the Vatican Website: http://w2.vatican.va/content/benedict-xvi/en.html[4]

Chapter Seventeen

Social Letters of Pope Francis, 2013-2015

THE JOY OF THE GOSPEL-*EVANGELII GAUDIUM,* 2013

"The Joy of the Gospel," fills the hearts and lives of all who encounter Jesus; it is joy ever new, a joy which is shared, and with Christ, joy is constantly born anew. In this very long exhortation, Pope Francis wishes to encourage the Christian faithful to embark upon a new chapter of evangelization marked by this joy, while pointing out new paths for the Church's journey in years to come.

This Letter addresses a huge amount of social problems, including the 'crisis of communal commitment,' the world markets, the economy of exclusion, inner city life, spiritual worldliness and consumerism, among other things. Today's world is pervaded by consumerism. Whenever our interior life becomes caught up in its own interests and concerns, there is no longer room for others, no place for the poor. Francis then invites all Christians, everywhere, at this very moment, to a renewed personal encounter with Jesus Christ whose Gospel, radiant with the glory of Christ's cross, constantly invites us to rejoice. Thanks solely to this encounter – or renewed encounter with God's love . . . we are liberated from our narrowness and self-absorption. Here we find the source and inspiration of all our efforts at evangelization, for if we have received the love which restores meaning to our lives, how can we fail to share that love with others? (EG #1-8).

Goodness always tends to spread. If we wish to lead a dignified and fulfilling life, we must reach out to others and seek their goodness. In this way, the Christian message will never grow old. We must always remember that evangelization is the Lord's work, and Jesus is the first and greatest evangelizer. Furthermore, we cannot forget that evangelization is first and foremost about preaching the Gospel to those who do not know Jesus or who have always rejected him.

In a conversational tone, Francis will then outline what he maintains are some guidelines which can encourage and guide the whole Church in a new phase of evangelization. In this part of the Letter, he will discuss the following questions:

a. The reform of the Church in her missionary outreach;
b. The temptations faced by pastoral workers;
c. The Church, understood as the entire People of God which evangelizes;
d. The homily and its preparation;
e. The inclusion of the poor in society;
f. Peace and dialogue within society;
g. The spiritual motivations for mission (EG #9-18).

God's word is unpredictable in its power. The Gospel speaks of a seed which once sown, grows by itself. The Church's closeness to Jesus is part of a common journey; communion and mission are profoundly interconnected. Evangelization consists mostly of patience and disregard for constraints of time. Faithful to the Lord's gift, it also bears fruit. Francis dreams of a "missionary option," capable of transforming everything, so that the Church's customs, ways of doing things, times and schedules, language and structures can be suitably channeled for the evangelization of today's world rather than for her self-preservation.

The parish continues to be "the Church living in the homes of her sons and daughters." It is the presence of the Church which provides an environment for hearing God's word, for growth in the Christian life, for dialogue, proclamation, charitable outreach, worship and celebration. The Bishop must always foster this missionary communion in his diocesan Church, following the ideal of the first Christian communities, in which the believers were of one heart and one soul. Francis must also think about a conversion of the papacy as he and the Bishops of the church need to hear the call to pastoral conversion (EG #19-33).

The pastoral message must concentrate on the essentials, on what is most beautiful, most grand, most appealing and, at the same time, most necessary. The saving love of God will always be central to the message. Works of love directed to one's neighbor are the most perfect external manifestation of the interior grace of the Spirit, and as far as external works are concerned, mercy is the greatest of all the virtues as Thomas Aquinas had stated.[1]

No one of the virtues can be excluded from the Christian ideal, so no truth may be denied. The integrity of the Gospel message must not be deformed, and each truth is better understood when related to the harmonious totality of the Christian message. When preaching is faithful to the Gospel, the centrality of certain truths is evident and it becomes clear that Christian morality is not a form of stoicism, or self-denial, or merely a practical philosophy or a catalogue of sins and faults (EG#34-39).

Today's vast and rapid cultural changes demand that we constantly seek ways of expressing unchanging truths in a language which brings out their abiding newness. "The deposit of the faith is one thing . . . the way it is expressed is another." The Church has rules or precepts which may have been quite effective in their time, but no longer have the same usefulness for directing and shaping people's lives. Evangelization operates within the limits of language and of circumstances. It constantly seeks to communicate more effectively the truth of the Gospel in a specific context, without renouncing the truth, the goodness and the light which it can bring whenever perfection is not possible. A missionary heart is aware of these limits and makes itself "weak with the weak . . . everything for everyone" (1 Cor. 9:22)[2] (EG #40-45).

The Church is called to be the house of the Father, with doors always wide open and a mother with an open heart. As in previous encyclicals, we are exhorted to an "ever watchful scrutiny of the signs of the times." Then Francis proceeds to talk about an economy of exclusion and inequality where a globalization of indifference has developed. Trickle-down theories which assume that economic growth, encouraged by a free market, will inevitably succeed in bringing about greater justice and inclusiveness in the world, have failed to produce.

Today's economic mechanisms promote inordinate consumption, yet it is evident that unbridled consumerism combined with inequality proves doubly damaging to the social fabric. Money has become an idol. The thirst for power and possessions knows no limits. Behind this attitude lurks a rejection of ethics and God. What is called for is an evangelization capable of shedding light on these new ways of relating to God, to others and to the world around us, and inspiring essential values. "The Joy of the Gospel," is such that it cannot be taken away from us by anyone or anything (cf. Jn. 16:22).[3] The evils of our world – and those of the Church – must not be excuses for diminishing our commitment and our fervor. We should be realists, but without losing our joy, our boldness, and our hope-filled commitment. Let us not allow ourselves to be robbed of missionary vigor (EG #46-109)!

Pope Francis will then state unequivocally that there can be no proclamation of the Gospel and no true evangelization without the explicit proclamation of Jesus as Lord, and without the primacy of the proclamation of Jesus Christ in all evangelizing work. In all the baptized, from first to last, the sanctifying power of the Spirit is at work, impelling us to evangelization.

In virtue of their Baptism, all the members of the People of God have become missionary disciples. Today, as the Church seeks to experience a profound missionary renewal, there is a kind of preaching which falls to each of us as a daily responsibility. It involves bringing the Gospel to the people we meet, whether they be our neighbors or complete strangers. Dialogue is much more than the communication of a truth. It arises from the enjoyment of speaking, and it enriches those who express their love for one another through the medium of words. The first step is calling upon the Holy Spirit in prayer (EG #110-175).

Francis discusses in detail: "The Social Dimension of Evangelization" because the task of evangelization implies and demands the integral promotion of each human being. In this section, much will be said concerning the Preferential Option for the Poor and a lack of Distributive Justice in society. This will be discussed in detail in the final section of this book.

The entirety of Section II of *Joy of the Gospel* deals with the *Inclusion of the Poor in Society.* Here, Pope Francis attacks the structural causes of poverty. He maintains that the financial system currently in place "rules and dominates," rather than," serves" humanity. It is a call to confront the evils of economic exclusion and injustice and a recommendation to immediately begin a process of structural reform. It is Francis' vision of an inclusive society:

> The need to resolve the structural causes of poverty cannot be delayed . . . As long as the problems of the poor are not radically resolved by rejecting the absolute autonomy of markets and financial speculation and by attacking the structural causes of inequality, no solution will be found for the world's problems or, for that matter, to any problems. Inequality is the root of social ills (EG #202).

Regarding the rights of the unborn and concern for their human dignity, Francis writes:

> Among the vulnerable for whom the Church wishes to care with love and concern particularly are unborn children, the most defenseless and innocent among us. Nowadays efforts are made to deny them their human dignity and to do with them whatever one pleases, taking their lives and passing laws preventing anyone from standing in the way of this (EG #213).

In the last part of his Letter, Francis addresses evangelization, dialogue, and social contact. He challenges the faithful to be "Spirit-filled evangelizers," fearlessly open to the working of the Holy Spirit and a people of prayer, while reminding us that we should always seek to be in union with the resurrected Jesus. Finally, he concludes this Letter by dedicating the work of evangelization to Mary, a model of evangelization and the Mother of the Church which evangelizes (EG #238-288).

This Letter can be found in its entirety at the Vatican Website: http://w2.vatican.va/content/francesco/en.html[4]

PRAISE BE: ON CARE FOR OUR COMMON HOME- *LAUDATO* SI, 2015

Pope Francis begins this Social Letter, "On Care for our Common Home," with the beautiful words of the Canticle of St. Francis of Assisi:

> "*LAUDATO SI', mi' Signore*" – "Praise be to you, my Lord."

To paraphrase Francis; Our Sister, Mother Earth, now cries out to us because of the harm we have inflicted on her by our irresponsible use and abuse of the goods of the earth graciously given to us. The sin in our hearts is reflected in the symptoms of sickness evident in the soil, in the water, in the air, and in all forms of life.

He then goes on to quote his predecessors, Paul VI, St. John Paul II, and Benedict XVI as well as Ecumenical Patriarch Bartholomew, in referring to their modern Letters on destruction of the environment.[5] These religious leaders all foresaw that there are ethical and spiritual roots of environmental problems. These environmental problems require that we look for solutions not only in technology but in a change of humanity. Otherwise we would be dealing merely with symptoms (LS #1-9).

Francis turns his attention to his inspirational namesake, Francis of Assisi, the patron saint of all who work in ecology. He uses him as a model for our loving of God's creation and for all those who see that our common home is being destroyed. He makes a personal appeal to bring the whole human family together to work together in building our common home. He particularly singles out those who recognize that the plight of environmental degradation weighs most heavily on the poorest of the world and asks for a new and open dialogue.

He ends this introduction by saying that in this letter he wishes to re-examine important questions, some of which have previously been dealt with by his predecessors. His examples include the intimate relationship between the poor and the fragility of the planet, the conviction that everything in the world is connected, the critique of new paradigms and forms of power derived from technology, the call to seek other ways of understanding the economy and progress, the value proper to each creature, the human meaning of ecology, the need for forthright and honest debate, the serious responsibility of international and local policy, the throwaway culture, and the proposal of a new lifestyle (LS #10-16).

The continued acceleration of changes affecting humanity and the planet is coupled today with a more intensified pace of life and work which Francis calls, "rapidification." (LS # 18) This is not necessarily geared to the common good or to sustainable human development. He then reviews some of the troubling questions facing humanity today:

1. Pollution and Climate Change

There are many pollutants affecting us today, but most especially the poor. They include atmospheric pollutants, high levels of smoke from cooking and heating fuels, transportation and industrial fumes, soil and water pollutants caused by fertilizers, insecticides and dangerous toxic waste. These problems are closely linked to what has become a "throwaway culture." Limiting use of these and moderating consumption are some alternative measures. Additionally, there is a disturbing warming of the climactic system which has resulted in rising sea levels and more extreme weather conditions. Greenhouse gases, fossil fuels, and deforestation have multiplied the problem. Melting of the polar ice caps has led to a dangerous release of methane gases. Changes in lifestyle, production, and consumption could possibly ameliorate all these. First and foremost, they affect the lives of the poor of the planet (LS #10-26).

2. The Issue of Water

Fresh drinking water is an issue of primary importance, since it is indispensable for human life. Demand exceeds the sustainable supply. Some countries have areas rich in water and waste it while others endure drastic scarcity. The quality of water available to the poor is a most serious problem resulting in many deaths, especially affecting infant mortality. Compounding this drinking water problem is the privatization of this valuable resource, turning it into a commodity subject to the laws of the marketplace. Scarcity of water will ultimately result in food and other resource price increases (LS #27-31).

3. Loss of Biodiversity

The earth's resources such as forests and woodlands are being plundered because of short-sighted approaches to the economy, commerce, and production. Each year sees the disappearance of thousands of plant and animal species which become extinct. Ecosystems are being destroyed and interventions are leading simply to the need for more interventions- some for better, others for worse. There is a need for far-sightedness, prohibitions, less waste and consumption, and a thorough studying of the problems. The earth's waters and marine life are being destroyed due to such things as pollution, uncontrolled fishing, destruction of marine organisms and coral reefs. Every intervention in nature can have consequences which are not immediately evident. Greater investment needs to be made in research to develop programs and strategies of protection to halt the loss of biodiversity (LS #32-42).

4. Decline in Quality of Human Life and the Breakdown of Society

Environmental Deterioration is having a dramatic effect on the quality of people's lives, especially the poor. Cities have become unhealthy to live in. The media and digital world are omnipresent. This contributes to a breakdown in the quality of real social relationships with others. They now tend to be replaced by a type of internet communication which enables us to choose or eliminate relationships at whim, thus giving rise to a new type of contrived emotion which has more to do with devices and displays than with other people and nature. People are not interacting with people as much as people are interacting with things (LS #43-47).

5. Global Inequality

The human environment and the natural environment deteriorate together. Francis will take up the issue of a lack of Distributive Justice not only here, but in several other parts of this Letter which will be discussed in Section Three, the final section of this book. Throughout the Letter, Francis ties many socio-economic problems to the environmental problems. Everything is closely interrelated, and today's problems call for a vision capable of accounting for every aspect of the global crisis for the common good. He maintains that environmental deterioration and human and ethical degradation are closely linked. Order and balance cannot be achieved without a concern particularly for distributive justice. The implication is that there can be no true social or economic justice, nor will there be peace on earth until humankind first makes peace with the earth. We must hear simultaneously, both the cry of the earth and the cry of the poor.

His suggested lines of approach to the multiplicity of problems outlined in his Letter include:

1. Prayerful reflection.
2. An economic-ecological integration.
3. Continuing dialogue on several fronts.
4. Recognition of scandalous levels of consumption.
5. A global solidarity and universal communion.
6. Changes in lifestyle.
7. Enforceable international agreements.
8. A transformation of the world's economies to be more inclusive of the poor.
9. Transparent political processes.
10. Ecological conversion and education.
11. A Christian spirituality that recognizes that while looking to heaven for guidance, for now we must walk the earth together. (LS # 216-220)

This Letter can be found in its entirety at the Vatican Website: http://w2.vatican.va/content/francesco/en.html[6]

Section Three: Distributive Justice and Distributism

Chapter Eighteen

Roots of Distributive Justice

THE BIBLE AND DISTRIBUTIVE JUSTICE

In addition to the modern papal letters which have formed Catholic Social Teaching since 1891, beginning with *(Rerum Novarum)*;[1] the Bible, from which much of this social teaching is drawn, has a lot to tell us in terms of distributive justice. In fact, most references to justice in the Bible are primarily to that of distributive justice.

In both the Old and New Testaments, the Bible never uses the terms "distributive justice" or even "social justice," but it does use the term "justice" many times in a variety of different contexts that refer to distributive justice particularly, and social justice generally. Concern for the poor, weak, and oppressed in society is a constant and recurring biblical theme which provides us with many examples of God's justice present in society. Here are just a few:

> He upholds the cause of the oppressed and gives food to the hungry. The Lord sets prisoners free, the Lord gives sight to the blind, the Lord lifts up those who are bowed down, the Lord loves the righteous (Psalm 146:7-8).[2]
>
> ***
>
> The righteous care about justice for the poor, but the wicked have no such concern (Prv. 29:7).[3]
>
> ***
>
> The Spirit of the Lord is upon me, because he has anointed me to bring glad tidings to the poor. He has sent me to proclaim liberty to captives and recovery of sight to the blind, to let the oppressed go free (Lk. 4:18).[4]

In the Bible, the intention of justice involves the proper distribution of goods, wealth, power and resources. Distributive justice takes on a character of restoration in a community building form using respect for human dignity and love of God and neighbor as its foundation. In so doing, it seeks to correct injustices and imbalances of material need. Distributive justice requires that preferential attention also be given to the poor, weak, oppressed, and marginalized, ex. (Mt. 25: 31-46; LK. 14:12-14; Lv. 19:10, 25:35-36; Prv. 31: 8-9,19:17; Ps. 72: 1-4; Jer. 22: 3-15).[5] This is done not simply to teach them how to cope with their poverty, weakness, oppression, or marginalization. Distributive justice seeks to remove these things from the society for the benefit of the common good. The implication created here, is that if we do not share our material wealth and other resources with those who are poor and disadvantaged, then we cannot really know God's love or God's justice in a biblical way.

If one looks first at the biblical story, beginning with creation and then the fall, reaching its high point in the incarnation and our redemption, and ending with Christ's return at the end of time and history, you find a continuous thread of socio-economic and spiritual life. Social life is ordered in such a way by God as to provide basic human dignity for every person created by God. Additionally, there are laws, commandments, proverbs and parables, stories, allegories, and propositions, as well as specific examples which require decisions. These are usually based on demonstrating God's love and God's justice.

Certainly, there are many references to all of the above that specify a fair and equitable distribution of society's goods, income, power, or resources. These are biblical references to the principle of distributive justice. They are all foundational for forming Catholic and Christian social teaching which revolve around socio-economic issues.

In the scriptures, there is seen to be only one Creator and owner of the earth and that is the Lord, our God. We are described as mere stewards and co-workers asked to use and equitably share the goods and resources of God's creation for the glory of God and to demonstrate our love both for God and neighbor. Because man is created in God's image, The Lord insists that we do this to insure basic respect for human dignity in all of society as well as for the benefit of the common good.

The earth must be seen to be more than simply a place for us to prepare ourselves for eternity. We are co-creators, co-workers, co-builders, and co-ad-"just"-ers with God while we are here on earth. Therefore, we cannot separate or compartmentalize the spiritual from the socio-economic. If we wish to show that God's love and God's justice dwells in us, then we must seek to love our neighbor and be willing to distribute more of our wealth and other resources to try to meet more of the basic needs of everyone in society. If we do this, distributive justice will not simply be either a biblical or a socio-economic term, but a living and present reality manifesting the love and justice of God at work in us and ultimately in society.

DISTRIBUTIVE JUSTICE IN ARISTOTLE'S *ETHICS AND POLITICS*

Aristotle wrote about many virtues in his *Ethics and Politics*, however, Justice is the only virtue to which he dedicated an entire book, Book V of *Nicomachean Ethics*.[6] To Aristotle, Justice was the most difficult of all the virtues because it was displayed toward others and not as much toward oneself. He considered it to be a perfect virtue because it was the practice of perfect virtue and thus was a social virtue. He argued that all other virtues become the virtue of Justice when they are used for the common good. To Aristotle, justice sought to secure people's rights and determined rewards and punishments.

Justice as a virtue, implied 'lawfulness' and 'fairness,' therefore laws encouraged people to be virtuous, so the just person, who was lawful and fair, would also be virtuous. As a virtue, he understood there to be two forms of justice, they were distributive justice and corrective justice. Corrective justice was actually a part of distributive justice.

Distributive justice dealt with the distribution of wealth, power, and other resources among the members of society, however, Aristotle first applied the principle to political authority. Corrective justice dealt with various remedies regarding uneven gain or loss between two people. Here, the gains and losses were equaled out to create a proper balance.

Injustice implied that things were out of balance, because one party had too much and another had too little. Additionally, Aristotle applied the principle of geometric proportionality to these forms of justice (Ex. In a two-party transaction, if one invests $1000 and another $100, profits should probably be divided on a ratio of 10:1 and not 50/50). Proportionality was just and what violated the proportion was unjust. Furthermore, he also maintained that greed was usually the operative vice to which injustice could be attributed.[7]

DISTRIBUTIVE JUSTICE IN MAIMONIDES *LAWS ON GIFTS FOR THE POOR; GUIDE FOR THE PERPLEXED*

Moses Maimonides, whose original name was Moses Ben Maimon, was the foremost intellectual figure of Medieval Judaism. He lived in Cordoba, Spain around one hundred years prior to the time St. Thomas Aquinas lived in Italy. What Aquinas' writings were to modern Christianity, Maimonides' writings became for modern Judaism.

His contributions in religion and philosophy have influenced Jewish and non-Jewish scholars alike. There are several works attributed to him including many commentaries on Jewish law. However, his *Guide for the Perplexed* [8] was his major life's work written over a period of fifteen years. Here are a few of the many things he had to say in his writings concerning distributive justice:

> Human beings have the privilege of distributing wealth the way that God intended. All wealth belongs to God, and it is up to the members of the community to distribute the wealth as God sees fit *(Laws on Gifts for the Poor, Treatise on Justice,* MM).[9]
>
> ***
>
> Another fundamental principle taught by the Law of Moses is this: Wrong cannot be ascribed to God in any way whatever; all evils and afflictions as well as all kinds of happiness of man, whether they concern one individual person or a community, are distributed according to justice; they are the result of strict judgment that admits no wrong (*Guide for the Perplexed*, MM, XVII, Fifth Theory, p.285).[10]

DISTRIBUTIVE JUSTICE IN THOMAS AQUINAS' *SUMMA THEOLOGICA*

Much of modern Catholicism, as well as modern Christianity, is indebted to Thomas Aquinas' *Summa*[11] . Conversely much of the theology which Aquinas formulated was almost entirely based on Aristotle's philosophy. St. Thomas had referred to Aristotle repeatedly as "the philosopher." Thomism attempted to synthesize Aristotelian philosophy with the principles of Christianity. Aquinas' *Summa* is footnoted in almost every modern Papal Social Letter we've reviewed previously which formed CST. Much of the theology put forth on distributive justice in the modern Papal Social Letters actually originated with Aquinas' theology and previously was taken from Aristotelian philosophy.

All justice, says Thomas Aquinas, orders man in relation to others. This can happen in two ways; the first with order in relation to individual men as such, and the other with order in relation to men as members of the community. The individual is always part of a larger society, and questions of justice or injustice must view man first from that standpoint.

To Thomas, distributive justice dealt with the relation of the community to individuals just as the whole has a relation to any part. In fact, *Summa, Section II, Q.61:1-4,*[12] pertaining to Aquinas' theology of distributive justice is quoted and referenced as a ground for Section# 33 of Pope Leo's *Rerum Novarum,*[13] which is seen to be the foundational document for Catholic Social Teaching. Distributive justice in *Rerum Novarum* will be discussed in the following chapter.

Unlike Aristotle, who maintained that greed was the operative vice that distributive injustices could be attributed to, Thomas Aquinas maintained that it was favoritism and/or prejudice (*Summa* Q.63:1-4).

DISTRIBUTIVE JUSTICE IN THE CATHOLIC CATECHISM

Human Solidarity

CC1940 Solidarity is manifested in the first place by the distribution of goods and remuneration for work. It also presupposes the effort for a more just social order where tensions are better able to be reduced and conflicts more readily settled by negotiation.

The Universal Destination and the Private Ownership of Goods

CC2402 "In the beginning, God entrusted the earth and its resources to the common stewardship of man-kind to take care of them, master them by labor, and enjoy their fruits. The goods of creation are destined for the whole human race. However, the earth is divided up among men to assure the security of their lives, endangered by poverty and threatened by violence. the appropriation of property is legitimate for guaranteeing the freedom and dignity of persons and for helping each of them to meet his basic needs and the needs of those in his charge. It should allow for a natural solidarity to develop between men."

CC2403 "The right to private property, acquired by work or received from others by inheritance or gift, does not do away with the original gift of the earth to the whole of mankind. the universal destination of goods remains primordial, even if the promotion of the common good requires respect for the right to private property and its exercise."

CC2404 "In his use of things man should regard the external goods he legitimately owns not merely as exclusive to himself but common to others also, in the sense that they can benefit others as well as himself. The ownership of any property makes its holder a steward of Providence, with the task of making it fruitful and communicating its benefits to others, his family first."

CC2405 "Goods of production - material or immaterial - such as land, factories, practical or artistic skills, oblige their possessors to employ them in ways that will benefit the greatest number. Those who hold goods for use and consumption should use them with moderation, reserving the better part for guests, for the sick and the poor."

Respect for Persons and their Goods

CC2411 "Contracts are subject to commutative justice which regulates exchanges between persons in accordance with a strict respect for their rights. Commutative justice obliges strictly; it requires safeguarding property rights, paying debts, and fulfilling obligations freely contracted. Without commutative justice, no other form of justice is possible. One distinguishes commutative justice from legal justice which concerns what the citizen owes in fairness to the community, and from distributive justice which regulates what the community owes its citizens in proportion to their contributions and needs."[14]

Chapter Nineteen

Distributive Justice in the Modern Papal Social Letters-The Foundational Letters

In the year 1891, as the world approached the turn of the century, several important world events were about to take place. In America, Benjamin Harrison had recently become the 23rd President and Liliuokalani was proclaimed queen of Hawaii that year as its last reigning monarch. Thomas Edison invented and patented the motion picture camera as well as the first electric radio, and the first gasoline powered automobile was about to revolutionize travel.

DISTRIBUTIVE JUSTICE-ON THE NEW THINGS

Across the ocean at the Vatican, "On the New Things," L. *Rerum Novarum,*[1] was about to appear on the world stage. It would be the first Social Encyclical authored by a pope and had been written to defend the struggling working classes of the world as well as to prioritize labor over capital and to stop the spread of atheistic Communism. *Rerum Novarum* was a watershed in the life of the modern Catholic Church because it placed the Church in the middle of the social, political and economic turmoil of the late nineteenth century. It also began a tradition of active engagement with the socio-economic order which slowly took shape over the next century. In writing this first Social Letter, Pope Leo would also lay the groundwork for the subsequent economic theory of Distributism. In the Letter, he made this landmark statement concerning distributive justice or the lack of it in society citing St. Thomas:

> It would be irrational to neglect one portion of the citizens and favor another, and therefore the public administration must solicitously provide for the welfare and the comfort of the working classes; otherwise, that law of justice will be violated which ordains that each man shall have his due. To cite the wise words of St. Thomas Aquinas: 'As the part and the whole are in a certain sense identical, so that which belongs to the whole in a sense belongs to the part.' Among the many duties of rulers who would do their best for the people, the first and chief is to act with strict justice—with that justice which is called distributive—toward each class alike (RN#33).

The subject of Distributive Justice would then be part of every Papal Social Letter which followed *Rerum Novarum* for the next one hundred years, up to and including the present day.

Distributism, as an economic theory, was never proposed by Pope Leo or any other of the modern Popes who would follow him in their Social Letters. It was a theory first brought forth by G.K. Chesterton and Hilaire Belloc[2] which was largely based on what was said concerning distributive justice by just two popes during the late 1800's and early 1900's. As stated previously, the first mention of distributive justice in these Social Letters was made by Pope Leo in the afore-mentioned document, *Rerum Novarum,* which ultimately became the foundation of what was to later come to be known as CST. The year 1931, forty years hence, saw the doubling of worldwide unemployment to 16.3%, and the world realized that the stock market crash of 1929 was having disastrous and far reaching effects. The gasoline powered automobile which was invented in 1891 had taken the world of travel by storm, but now many car manufacturers were going out of business as people did not have money to buy new cars, let alone afford gasoline at the unbelievably high price of 10 cents per gallon.

DISTRIBUTIVE JUSTICE-ON THE FORTIETH YEAR

In 1931, there entered a second Pope who would influence Chesterton and Belloc's economic theory of Distributism. On the fortieth anniversary of the first Social Letter, a new Social Encyclical was presented to the world to celebrate the issuance of *Rerum Novarum.* This one was simply called, "On the Fortieth Year, L. *Quadragessimo Anno,*[3] and was authored by Pope Pius XI. This Letter as its subtitle indicated dealt with the "Reconstruction of the Social Order."

It made more of a contribution than the first Letter in discussing the lack of distributive justice in society at length. It spoke about the unmerited poverty of non-owning workers, and the enormous injustice and inequality in the distribution of this world's goods, which could in no way conform to the designs of the all-wise Creator. It maintained that the distribution of property and wealth in the world had not reached the satisfactory degree of perfection which God intended. Furthermore, that the distribution among individual persons and classes for the common good of all in society, which Pope Leo had praised, was not being safeguarded. The Letter indicated that by this law of social justice, one class should not be excluding the other from sharing in the benefits of a just distribution. Hence, the class of the wealthy violated this law no less, when by its wealth, it thought that it was the right order of things for it to get everything and the worker nothing.

The Letter outlined that each, therefore, must be given his own share of goods, and it championed the just distribution of created goods. It maintained that it was one of the gravest evils existing in the current society for there to be a huge disparity between the few exceedingly rich and the unnumbered property-less. This must be brought into conformity with the norms of the common good, that is, social justice. The riches which were so abundantly produced in this the "Industrial Age," as it was called, are not being rightly distributed and equitably made available to the various classes of people. The people of this age with all their strength and effort should be striving, so that at least in the future the abundant fruits of production will accrue equitably to those who are rich and then will be distributed in ample sufficiency among the workers.

The only way in which society will be renewed and reconstructed so that the distribution of goods will become a just distribution will be for men to return openly and sincerely to the teaching of the Gospel. The result of this, will be that economic life will be led back to sound and right order for the common good of all in society. If these principles are observed by everyone, not only the production and acquisition of goods, but also the use of wealth, which now is seen to be so often contrary to right order, will be brought back soon within the bounds of equity and just distribution.

Throughout the Letter, on no less than seven separate occasions, Pius will talk about "inequality in the distribution of this world's goods," and "just distribution," (QA #5, 57, 58, 60, 61, 76, 136).[4] These are his references to "distributive justice." A few examples of these are:

"The same feeling those many Catholics, both priests and laymen, shared, whom a truly wonderful charity had long spurred on to relieve the unmerited poverty of the non-owning workers, and who could in no way convince themselves that so enormous and unjust an inequality in the distribution of this world's goods truly conforms to the designs of the all-wise Creator (QA #5)."

***

To each, therefore, must be given his own share of goods, and the distribution of created goods, which, as every discerning person knows, is laboring today under the gravest evils due to the huge disparity between the few exceedingly

> rich and the unnumbered property-less, must be... brought into conformity with the norms of the common good, that is, social justice (QA #58).
>
> ***
>
> If these principles are observed by everyone, everywhere, and always, not only the production and acquisition of goods but also the use of wealth, which is seen to be so often contrary to right order, will be brought back soon within the bounds of equity and just distribution (QA #136).

Although G.K. Chesterton had been influenced in writing his economic theory of Distributism by only these two Popes, Leo and Pius, there would be five more Popes, thirteen more Social Letters, one church Council, and several Bishops up to today who would raise their voices to proclaim the lack of distributive justice in society and the need for reconstruction of the social order. These would all form the basis for the body of theology that is called CST today.

During his papacy, Pius would author thirty-three more Papal Letters, however only one would deal with the social ills of the world, "On the Fortieth Year," L. *Quadragesimo Anno*. The others would address doctrine, dogma, and other insular matters of the church. Following Pius XI's Social Letter, another 30 years would pass. During the ensuing years 1961-1963, as the world moved away from World War II and was then on the brink of World War III and a nuclear war, a new Pope, John XXIII would author two Social Letters. These dealt specifically with the ills of society, and recommended reconstruction of the social order. They were called, "Mother and Teacher," L. *Mater et Magistra*[5], and "Peace on Earth," L. *Pacem in Terris*.[6] Although both Letters dealt with a broad spectrum of social issues, they also had much to add to the ongoing call for distributive justice in society.

Chapter Twenty

Distributive Justice in the Social Letters of Pope John XXIII; and Vatican Council II

DISTRIBUTIVE JUSTICE IN MOTHER AND TEACHER

Pope John XXIII's first Letter, "Mother and Teacher," L. *Mater et Magistra*,[1] was written in 1961. As its subtitle suggested, it was written to measure "Christianity and Social Progress." At the time, society viewed work as a commodity. The Letter issued a call for a new mindset which viewed work more in terms of a specifically human activity. Remuneration for work should not depend on the state of the market, but as being determined by the laws of justice and equity. Any other procedure would be a clear violation of justice.

The state was seen to have a role in insuring this in accordance with justice and to safeguard the human dignity of all workers. The first two Social Letters, Pope Leo's *Rerum Novarum*[2] *and* Pope Pius' *Quadragesimo Anno*[3] would be given credit for launching a new branch of jurisprudence which was then called, "Labor Law" (MM # 21; QA # 35).

The Letter reaffirmed that all forms of economic enterprise must be governed by the principles of social justice and charity and that all economic activity should be conducted not merely for private gain but also in the interests of the common good. In quoting the first Social Letter of Pope Leo in 1891, this letter also reaffirmed that the right to the private possession of material goods is admittedly a natural one; nevertheless, in the objective order established by God, the right to property cannot stand in the way of the axiomatic principle that "the goods which were created by God for all men should flow to all according to the principles of justice and charity" (MM # 40, 43).

There are references to a disregard for distributive justice in society in no less than seven sections of the Letter (MM#48, 74, 82-83, 113-115, 136, 168).[4] Some examples are:

> . . . The economic prosperity of a nation is not so much its total assets in terms of wealth and property, as the equitable division and distribution of this wealth (MM#74).
>
> ***
>
> Justice is to be observed not only in the distribution of wealth, but also according to the conditions in which men are engaged in producing this wealth (MM#82).
>
> ***
>
> . . . However, it is no less necessary—and justice itself demands—that the riches produced be distributed fairly among all members of the political community (MM# 168).

Pius' Encyclical, *Quadragesimo Anno* was also given due credit here for, its guiding Principle of Subsidiary. This was termed as a fundamental principle of social philosophy, unshaken and unchangeable. . . "Just as it is wrong to withdraw from the individual and commit to a community what private enterprise and industry can accomplish, so too it is an injustice, a grave evil and a disturbance of right order, for a larger and higher association to arrogate to itself functions which can be performed efficiently by smaller and lower societies. The true aim of all social activity should be to help members of the social body, but never to destroy or absorb them (QA # 53; MM # 117)."

Regarding the structure of industry, justice is to be observed not only in the distribution of wealth, but also according to the conditions in which men are engaged in producing this wealth. Every man has, of his very nature, a need to express himself in his work and thereby to perfect his own being. The International Labor Organization—known in various countries as the O.I.L. or I.L.O. Or O.I.T. should be given due recognition for making an effective and valued contribution to the establishment in the world of an economics and social order marked by justice and humanity, an order which was seen to safeguard the lawful rights of the working man (QA # 5, 58, 76; MM # 103).

Justice itself demands that the riches produced be distributed fairly among all members of the political community. This means that everything must be done to ensure that social progress keeps pace with economic progress. Every sector of the economy—agriculture, industry and the services—must progress evenly and simultaneously. Justice also demands that all such technical and financial aid be given without thought of domination, but to help the less developed nations to achieve their own economic and social growth. (MM # 168)

Finally, this Social Letter closes by stating that the church is the "Mother and Teacher" of all nations. "Mercy and truth have met each other: justice and peace have kissed. Truth is sprung out of the earth: and justice hath looked down from heaven. For the Lord will give goodness: and our earth shall yield her fruit. Justice shall walk before him: and shall set his steps in the way (MM # 262)."

DISTRIBUTIVE JUSTICE IN PEACE ON EARTH

The second Letter, "Peace on Earth," L. *Pacem in Terris*,[5] was written in 1963. It sought to establish universal peace in truth, justice, charity, and liberty. It opens by discussing a series of mutual rights and duties. These rights pertain to moral and cultural values, the freedom to worship God according to one's conscience, the right to choose one's state in life, economic rights, right of meeting and association, the right to emigrate and immigrate, and political rights. These rights will be determined in accordance with the precepts of justice and will be guided by it. The rights are bound up with a series of duties which derive their origin, sustenance, and their indestructability from natural law. In human society, one man's right will give rise to a corresponding duty in other men.

This Letter will stress the importance of the existence of justice in society and the need for states to be regulated by justice in their relations with one another. To not adhere to this principle is to give rise to what St Augustine warned against, "Take away justice, and what are kingdoms but mighty bands of robbers."[6] Solidarity is also stressed since relationships between States must be regulated in accordance with the principles of truth and justice. States must further these relationships by taking positive steps to pool their material and spiritual resources. This can be achieved by mutual collaboration in the economic, social, political, educational, health and athletic spheres.

In this Letter, Pope John doesn't say anything about "distributive justice," in those words particularly, but he does use language which discusses a sharing of the world's goods. For example, he maintains that we have a responsibility and are duty bound to:

> . . . share our goods with others (PT #35).
> . . . share our enjoyment of all the wholesome pleasures of the world (PT #36).
> . . . share in every sector of human society: in the socio-economic sphere, in government, and in the realm of learning and culture (PT #40).

And:

> It is the nature of the common good that every citizen has the right to share in it (PT # 56).

At the heart of the Letter is the call for "Peace on Earth." Nuclear weapons must be banned. This necessitates disarmament as justice, right reason, and the recognition of man's dignity cry out insistently for a cessation to the arms race. Any disputes which may arise between nations must be resolved by negotiation and agreement, and not by recourse to arms. This conviction owes its origin chiefly to the terrifying destructive force of modern weapons. It arises from fear of the ghastly and catastrophic consequences of their use. Thus, in this age which boasts of its atomic power, it no longer makes sense to maintain that war is a fit instrument with which to repair the violation of justice. Each one of us is required to make his own contribution to the universal common good. Daily, there exists the need to make the reality of social life conform better to the requirements of justice. Furthermore, the cost of stockpiling nuclear weapons has been achieved at the expense of the oppression of poorer, less developed nations.

Finally, we should pray with all fervor for this peace which our divine Redeemer came to bring us. May He banish from the souls of men whatever might endanger peace. May He transform all men into "witnesses of truth, justice and brotherly love (PT # 171)."

VATICAN COUNCIL II

In 1962, Pope John would throw open wide the windows of the church as an effort to let the Holy Spirit in. The Pope would call this, an *Aggiornamento,* which he saw as a freshening of thinking and practices that would better enable the Church to do God's work and serve the whole people of God on earth. To do this, he would call only the Second Vatican Council the church had ever had in St. Peter's Basilica. The previous Vatican Council had occurred nearly a century before. This one would last for three years from 1962-1965 and the purpose of this council was to be a liberalization and modernization of the practices of the church. It would also seek to move the church away from the Triumphalist Church of the last century and into being what it was called to be, "The Church in the Modern World."

Vatican II spanned two papacies, first that of John XXIII who convened the Council, and Paul VI who succeeded him. By custom they did not normally attend the working sessions of the Council: John XXIII opened the Council, and Paul VI closed it. There were 2500 Council Fathers who were mainly of Episcopal rank, to include Bishops, Cardinals, and Superiors of Male Religious Orders. There were over 3000 theologians, academics, and other ecclesial experts who played an invaluable role in shaping debates and the ensuing documents which came forth from the Council. As guests, many senior members of other Christian denominations were invited to the Council as observers and proved invaluable in several private discussions. They could not, however, join in Council debates or participate in the voting.

At Vatican II, 16 Documents in all were generated; 4 were considered Constitutions, 3 Declarations, and 9 Decrees. Of the many important documents that came from this council, two were considered Social Letters of the church and incorporated into that part of Moral Theology which is now referred to as CST. These two were the "Document on Religious Freedom;" L. *Dignitatis Humanae,*[7] and Pastoral Constitution on the Church, L. *Gaudium et Spes.*[8]

DISTRIBUTIVE JUSTICE IN THE DOCUMENT ON RELIGIOUS FREEDOM

As one of the 3 Declarations released by the Council, The Document on Religious Freedom, *Dignitatis Humanae* was almost totally focused on religious freedom and the council attempted to establish it as being grounded in the human dignity of man who is made in the image of God. The necessity of religious freedom is most certainly an important facet of CST, as human dignity is one of the central themes of this theology. The document, however, makes no mention of the need for distributive justice in society; neither does the document discuss distributive injustice. Therefore, for our purposes, because distributive justice is the focus of this section, we will not discuss this document any further. The Document on Religious Freedom as part of CST, has already been discussed at length in Section Two of this book.

DISTRIBUTIVE JUSTICE IN THE PASTORAL CONSTITUTION ON THE CHURCH

The Pastoral Constitution on the Church, *Gaudium et Spes,* was one of only four major and extensive documents issued at Vatican II that was to be rightly called a "Constitution." It is also considered to be an important Social Letter of the church as this document is a complete overview of the human person's relationship to society.

In many documents issued by the church over the last century there had been a "turning inward," so that the church could view herself and her position in the world. The Pastoral Constitution on the Church turns this around in much the same way that the altar was turned around at Vatican II. Right from the beginning, in the document's Introductory Statement, the Pastoral Constitution states that it will "View the Situation of Men in the Modern World." As it does this it finds that there has never been such an abundance of wealth, resources, and economic power in the world. (GS # 4)

Yet it also finds that there exists much in the way of a lack of distributive justice because a huge proportion of the worlds citizens are still tormented by hunger and poverty. Furthermore, countless numbers still suffer from total illiteracy. There are also new forms of social and psychological slavery which have made their appearance. The people of the world are most grievously torn into opposing camps by conflicting forces. Political, social, economic, racial and ideological disputes continue to fester and are rapidly on the rise. (GS # 4, 60)

Further on in this Document, in highlighting this world abundance of wealth, resources, and economic power, with the ensuing lack of distributive justice that goes along with it, the Church will declare that:

> God intended the earth with everything contained in it for the use of all human beings and peoples. Thus, under the leadership of justice and in the company of charity, created goods should be in abundance for all in like manner . . . man should regard the external things that he legitimately possesses not only as his own but also as common in the sense that they should be able to benefit not only him but also others (GS # 69).

There are seen to be some problems of special urgency which must be discussed. They pertain to marriage and the family, human progress, life in its economic, social and political dimensions, the bonds between the family of nations, and peace. Therefore, the church, in her role, can first offer guidance and support to those who are trying to preserve the holiness and to foster the natural dignity of the married state and proclaim and defend marriage and family life and its superlative value. The church can also assist in the proper development of human culture by always reminding society that human culture should be subordinated to the integral perfection of the human person, to the good of the community and of the whole society. It will always seek to harmonize human culture with Christian culture whenever possible.

Regarding distributive justice, the Letter does address economic development. The church believes that it must remain under man's determination. It should not be left to the judgment of a few men or groups possessing too much economic power or of the political community alone or of certain more powerful nations. For example:

> As a result, many persons are quite aggressively demanding those benefits of which with vivid awareness they judge themselves to be deprived either through injustice or unequal distribution (GS #9).

And:

> To satisfy the demands of justice and equity, strenuous efforts must be made, without disregarding the rights of persons or the natural qualities of each

country, to remove as quickly as possible the immense economic inequalities, which now exist and are connected to individual and social discrimination (GS #66).

In stressing the need for Solidarity as a possible initial step toward a solution for this dichotomy of distributive justice, the Church recommends that:

"Christians should cooperate willingly and wholeheartedly in establishing an international order that includes a genuine respect for all freedoms and amicable brotherhood between all . . . Do not let men, then, be scandalized because some countries, with most citizens who are counted as Christians, have an abundance of wealth, whereas others are deprived of the necessities of life and are tormented with hunger, disease, and every kind of misery. The spirit of poverty and charity are the glory and witness of the Church of Christ (GS # 88)."

The Document makes note that the Church recognizes that many nations on the road to progress, desire to participate in the goods of modern civilization, not only politically but also economically. In recognition of their inherent human dignity, many people are now demanding those benefits of which they judge themselves to be deprived either through injustice or unequal distribution. Although rightful differences exist between men, the equal dignity of persons demands that a more humane and just condition of life be brought about. For excessive economic and social differences between the members of the one human family or population groups cause scandal, and militate against social justice. To satisfy the demands of justice and equity, strenuous efforts must be made to remove as quickly as possible the immense economic inequalities, which now exist, and in many cases, are growing. For its part, the Church with its vast deposit of faith, needs to prove its fruitfulness:

"by penetrating the believer's entire life, including its worldly dimensions, and by activating him toward justice and love, especially regarding the needy (GS # 21)."

Finally, a very important statement on the need for distributive justice in society is made in this Document. It is somewhat hidden as it is made after the Document concludes and is tucked away in a relatively obscure footnote to it. Footnote # 10 gives attribution to an earlier statement made by John XXIII in a radio-television message he gave to the people of the world on September 11, 1962. In it, Pope John said as follows:

The obligation of every man, the urgent obligation of the Christian man, is to reckon what is superfluous by the measure of the needs of others, and to see to it that the administration and the distribution of created goods serve the common good.[9]

Chapter Twenty-One

Distributive Justice in the Social Letters of Pope Paul VI

DISTRIBUTIVE JUSTICE IN THE PROGRESS OF PEOPLES

In 1967, a few years after the closing of the Vatican Council, Pope Paul VI authored a new Social Letter titled "The Progress of Peoples," L. *Populorem Progressio.*[1] The Letter pertained to the progressive development of peoples. It focused particularly on those who are trying to escape the ravages of hunger, poverty, disease and ignorance. It also highlighted those who are seeking a larger share in the benefits of civilization.

To try to accomplish more in distributing goods justly and equitably, Pope Paul recommended the creation of a new pontifical commission, to be called "The Justice and Peace Commission." The role of this commission will be to assist the less developed nations of the world to contribute to their own development through the pooling of ideas and activities. The name of the commission was seen to be an apt description of the commission's program and its goal. (PP # 5)

It will be the first time, however, within the growing body of theology contained in CST that integral human development as a holistic concept would appear. It will also be the first time that distributive justice would be placed within an international context. The Letter states just what the crux of the problem is:

> The hungry nations of the world cry out to the peoples blessed with abundance. The Church, cut to the quick by this cry, asks each man to hear his brother's plea and answer it lovingly (PP #3).

The poor in the underdeveloped nations are suffering the most. The economy of the world should serve mankind and not just the chosen few. The Catholic Church, many Christians, and people of good will believe that there are moral imperatives because of the uneven and unjust distribution of wealth and material resources. The remedy appears to be some form of greater distributive justice and a sharing of the wealth of developed nations. For example:

> . . . these structures are no match for the harsh economic realities of today...the disparity between rich and poor nations will increase rather than diminish; the rich nations are progressing with rapid strides while the poor nations move forward at a slow pace. The imbalance grows with each passing day: while some nations produce a food surplus, other nations are in desperate need of food...(PP#8).

And:

> No one may appropriate surplus goods solely for his own private use when others lack the bare necessities of life (PP #23).

Also:

> The injustice of certain situations cries out for God's attention. Lacking the bare necessities of life, whole nations are under the thumb of others . . . injustices must be challenged and overcome . . . It is not enough to increase the general fund of wealth and then distribute it more fairly (PP #30-34).

The primary issue is seen to be what the recent Vatican Council reiterated as truth: "God intended the earth and everything in it for the use of all human beings and peoples. Thus, under the leadership of justice and in the company of charity, created goods should flow fairly to all." All other rights, whatever they may be, including the rights of property and free trade, are to be subordinated to this principle. (PP # 22)

To correct these distributive injustices from occurring most particularly within the poorest of nations, a program of reform is recommended as one which is preferable to that of revolution. Programs of the past which have favored revolution as the answer to these injustices have only proven to engender new injustices, introduce new inequities, and bring new disasters. Evil situations that exist, should not be dealt with in such a way that an even worse situation is the result. (PP # 29-31)

There should be a joint effort of all nations of the world to assist in the development of humanity for the common good. But, the wealthier nations of the world have three major duties to accomplish this: First, the wealthier nations have an obligation which stems from the universal human and supernatural brotherhood of man to be in mutual solidarity with the poorer nations through giving aid to developing nations. Secondly, as a matter of social justice, the wealthier nations should rectify any inequities and imbalances in trade relations between strong and weak nations. Third, wealthier nations should be committed to universal charity to build a more humane world community. There is a need to build a world community where all can give and receive, and where the progress of some is not brought about at the expense of others. (PP # 44)

To bring about distributive justice at every level, the first Catholic Social Letter of Pope Leo XIII, *Rerum Novarum,*[2] is cited as having a formula to correct situations when two nations are in very unequal positions in a contract which is rendered as unfair and unjust. Trade relations can no longer be based solely on the principle of free, unchecked competition which creates an economic dictatorship. Free trade can only be considered "just" when it conforms to the demands of social justice. (PP # 59-61)

Self-interest and profit at another's expense should not be the primary and only consideration when a wealthier nation seeks to do business with a less developing nation. This should also apply to large businesses when contracting to conduct business in a less developed nation. Justice should prevail. (PP # 5, 48, 57)

Each man should seek the betterment of the other out of brotherly love. All men of deep thought and wisdom are called to consider these words. Those who have heard the cries of the people of needy nations who call out for justice daily are the promoters and apostles of genuine progress and true development. Genuine progress does not consist in wealth sought for personal comfort or for its own sake; rather it consists in an economic order designed for the welfare of all human persons who reflect the glow of brotherly love. (PP# 86)

DISTRIBUTIVE JUSTICE-ON THE EIGHTIETH YEAR

1971 saw the eightieth birthday of the first Catholic Social Letter, *Rerum Novarum.*[3] During this anniversary year, Pope Paul VI issued a new Catholic Social Letter, not only to celebrate the original Letter's birthday, but to keep both the old and new social problems of the world continually in the minds of humanity. During 1971, Pope Paul authored what was to be only his second Social Letter, On the Eightieth Year, L. *Octagesima Adveniens.*[4]

This pope had travelled extensively during his papacy and saw firsthand the evidence of much injustice being done to people in developing and underdeveloped nations. The Letter outlines the fact that there is an urgent need to establish a greater justice in the sharing of goods, both within national communities and on the international level. Distributive justice is seen to be a top priority. In international exchange, there is a need to go beyond relationships based on force to arrive at agreements reached with the good of all in mind. Relationships based on force and coercion have never in fact established justice in a true and lasting manner. The use of force fosters a climate of struggle which opens the way to situations of extreme violence and abuse. (OA # 43)

Once again, the problems in much of the world can be attributed to an inequality and injustice in the distribution of goods. There exists a total disregard for distributive justice.

For example:

> Flagrant inequalities exist in the economic, cultural and political development of the nations: . . . while some countries enjoy prosperity, others are struggling against starvation (OA #2).

And:

> These problems include . . . fairness in the exchange of goods and in the division of wealth (OA #7).

Also:

> There is a need to establish a greater justice in the sharing of goods, both within national communities and on the international level (OA #42-43).

What is necessary is a complete change of men's attitudes and a change of the structures in society which perpetuate the injustices. Today men yearn to free themselves from need and dependence. But this liberation starts with the interior freedom that men must find with their goods, their resources, and their power; they will never reach it except through a transcendent love for humankind and a solidarity which arises within the brotherhood of man. The most revolutionary ideologies lead only to a change of masters; once they obtain their power, these new masters want to surround themselves with privileges, limit the freedom of others, and then allow other forms of injustice to become established. Trading one set of injustices for another will never bring justice to society. Hence, many people are reaching the point of questioning the very model of society. (OA # 45)

The competition between highly developed, wealthier, and more powerful nations sets them in opposition in the race to attain greater technological, economic and military power. This, in and of itself, stands in the way of setting up structures in which progress would be regulated with a view to greater social justice and equity in the overall distribution of the world's goods.

Laymen, in particular, are assigned the task to renew the temporal order. If the role of the hierarchy is to teach and to interpret authentically the norms of morality to be followed in this matter, it belongs to the laity, without waiting passively for orders and directives, to take the initiatives freely and to infuse a Christian spirit into the mentality, customs, laws and structures of the community in which they are living. (OA # 48)

Let each one search his soul to see what he has done up to now, and what he ought to do. It is not enough to simply cry out at injustices and utter prophetic denunciations; these words will lack real import unless they are accompanied for each of us by an awareness of personal responsibility and by effective action. Words must be supported with action and deeds. It is too easy to point the finger at others and their responsibility for injustice. Each one must realize how they share in it personally, and how a personal metanoia is needed first. The task can be viewed as limitless in size without the aid of the Holy Spirit. Our Christian hope comes primarily from the fact that we know that the Lord is working with us to bring justice to the structures and institutions of society in the world. He continues to do this by rising in his Body which is the Church - and, through the Church, in renewing all of humanity. (OA # 50-52)

Chapter Twenty-Two

Distributive Justice in the Social Letters of Pope John Paul II, 1981-1991

DISTRIBUTIVE JUSTICE IN THROUGH WORK

Through Work, L. *Laborem Exercens*,[1] was the first Social Letter authored by Pope John Paul II. It was issued in the year 1981 to celebrate the 90th anniversary of *Rerum Novarum*.[2] In the Letter, John Paul will look at human work as a dimension of all that is human. Almost from the beginning of this Letter, the concept of distributive justice will be made an intricate part of the entirety of his discussion which concerns human work.

John Paul sees many new hopes in society today, but also new fears connected with work as a basic dimension of human existence. There is a special dignity which work encompasses, but it also contains much of the injustice which penetrates social life both within individual nations and on an international level. The question of social and distributive justice has moved to a higher plateau as during the times of the writing of *Rerum Novarum and Quadragesimo Anno,*[3] it was a matter of injustices within individual nations. Now, its horizon takes in the spectrum of the whole world and it is far more prevalent and more complex. To build and achieve social and distributive justice on the earth, unjust structures and institutions can no longer be concealed, but must be examined. Injustices have reached the point where they cry out to heaven and justice demands that they be transformed on a universal scale. (LE # 2)

Rapid industrialization was seen to be justified from the point of view of social morality. This was favored by the liberal socio-political system, which in accordance with its "economistic" premises, strengthened and safeguarded economic initiative by the possessors of capital alone. But the possessors of capital have not paid sufficient attention to the rights of the workers. This has occurred because human work has heretofore been viewed solely as an instrument of production, and capital; the basis and purpose of production. (LE # 7-13)

To move away from this distorted worldview, worker solidarity, together with a clearer understanding of workers' rights, has in many cases brought about profound changes. Today, workers can often share in running businesses and in controlling their productivity through appropriate associations. But at the same time, various ideological or power structures have arisen at various levels of society, to allow flagrant social injustices to persist or have created new ones. On the world level, new forms of social and distributive injustice, much more extensive than those which in the last century have only stimulated unity and solidarity between workers. (LE # 8, 20)

To achieve greater social justice in the various parts of the world, and in the relationship between various countries, there is a need for ever new movements of solidarity of the workers and with the workers. This solidarity must be present whenever it is called for by the social degrading of the subject of work, by exploitation of the workers, and by the growing areas of poverty and hunger. The Church is firmly committed to this cause, for she considers it her mission, her service, a proof of her fidelity to Christ, so that she can truly be the "Church of the Poor." (LE # 8)

The distributive justice or injustice inherent in any socio-economic system, deserves in the final analysis to be evaluated by the way in which man's work is properly remunerated in the system. Here we return once more to the first principle of the whole ethical and social order, namely, the principle of the common use of goods. In every system, regardless of the fundamental relationships within it between capital and labor, wages are still a practical means whereby many people can have access to those goods which are intended for common use; both the goods of nature and manufactured goods. Both kinds of goods become accessible to the worker through the wage which he receives as remuneration for his work. Hence, in every case, a just wage is the concrete means of verifying the justice of the whole socio-economic system and is a check and balance that it is functioning justly. It is not the only means of checking, but it is a particularly important one and, in a sense, the key means. (LE # 18-19)

Both the Sacred Scriptures and The Second Vatican Council have confirmed that work is a sharing in the activity of the Creator. Man has been created in God's image and has received a mandate to subject to himself, the earth and all that it contains, and to govern the world with justice and holiness. Such a vision of the values of human work can also be viewed as a spirituality of work. This also explains the right meaning of progress: "A person is more precious for what he is than for what he has. Similarly, all that people do to obtain greater justice, wider brotherhood, and a more humane ordering of social relationships has greater worth than all the technical advances. For these advances can supply the material for human progress, but of themselves alone they can never actually bring it about." (LE # 26)

If one continues to study the development of the question of social justice, it can clearly be seen that the disproportionate distribution of wealth and poverty, along with the existence of some countries and continents that are developed and of others that are not, calls for a just levelling out and for a search for new ways to ensure just development for all. (LE # 2)

DISTRIBUTIVE JUSTICE IN THE SOCIAL CONCERN OF THE CHURCH

The Social Concern of the Church-L. *Sollicitudo Rei Socialis*,[4] was authored by Pope John Paul II in the year 1987. This Social Letter is directed towards an authentic development of man and society which would respect and promote all the dimensions of the human person.

From an economic point of view, the developing countries are much more numerous than the developed ones. The result of this is that the billions of human beings who lack the goods and services offered by development are far more prevalent than those who possess them. This has created a very serious problem of unequal distribution of the means of subsistence originally meant for everybody. Thus, an unequal distribution of the benefits deriving from these goods has also occurred. This all happens not through the fault of the poor people of the developing and underdeveloped countries. (SS # 9)

The fact that the social question has acquired a worldwide dimension, necessitates that the demand for distributive justice can only be satisfied on that level. If the demand for justice is unheeded and ignored, then this could encourage the temptation among the victims of injustice to respond with violence, as happens at the origin of many wars.

The many people excluded from the equitable distribution of the goods originally destined for all which would benefit the common good, could ask themselves: why not respond with violence to those who have first treated us with violence? This is not to conclude that violence is a good solution to the distributive injustices, but only that violence does in fact occur as a perceived solution by the victims of distributive injustice. In a different world, ruled by concern for the common good of all humanity, rather than for the quest for individual profit, peace would indeed be possible as the result of a more perfect justice among people. (SS # 10, 39)

In looking at the peoples of the world as one whole body of humanity, one can see an ever-widening gap between the so-called developed North and the developing South. This geographical terminology is only an indication, since one cannot ignore the fact that the frontiers of wealth and poverty intersect within the societies themselves, whether developed or developing. Social inequalities and distributive injustices in the production and distribution of goods and resources is scandalous wherever and however it occurs. (SS # 14-15)

In his view, John Paul perceives that it is the injustice of the poor distribution of the goods and resources originally intended for all, and the complete disregard for the common good of all humankind that is one of the central issues existent within society. (SS # 10, 28) There is much said about distributive injustice as economic injustice in the Letter. John Paul raises here, the inequality of the distribution of goods among developed and developing nations and people. Much injustice in distribution exists worldwide, but particularly between the developed North and the undeveloped South. For example:

"We are therefore faced with a serious problem of unequal distribution of the means of subsistence originally meant for everybody, and thus also an unequal distribution of the benefits deriving from them (SS #9)." And:

> . . . how can one justify the fact that huge sums of money, which could and should be used for increasing the development of peoples, are instead utilized for the enrichment of individuals or groups, or assigned to the increase of stockpiles of weapons, both in developed countries and in the developing ones, thereby upsetting the real priorities? This is even more serious given the difficulties which often hinder the direct transfer of capital set aside for helping needy countries. If 'development is the new name for peace,' war and military preparations are the major enemy of the integral development of peoples (SS #10).

Also:

> The abundance of goods and services available in some parts of the world, particularly in the developed North, is matched in the South by an unacceptable delay, and it is precisely in this geopolitical area that the major part of humanity lives (SS #14).

> . . . peace is indivisible. It is either for all or for none. It demands an even greater degree of rigorous respect for justice and consequently a fair distribution of the results of true development (SS#26).

> This then is the picture: there are some people - the few who possess much - who do not really succeed in 'being' because, through a reversal of the hierarchy of values, they are hindered by the cult of 'having'; and there are others - the many who have little or nothing - who do not realize their basic human vocation because they are deprived of essential goods (SS #28).

> One of the greatest injustices in the contemporary world consists precisely in this: that the ones who possess much are relatively few and those who possess almost nothing are many. It is the injustice of the poor distribution of the goods and services originally intended for all (SS# 28).

DISTRIBUTIVE JUSTICE IN THE ONE HUNDREDTH YEAR

The One Hundredth Year-L. *Centessimus Annus,*[5] was authored by John Paul II in 1991 to commemorate the one hundred years that had passed since the writing of the foundational document, *Rerum Novarum*[6] in the year 1891. Coincidentally, it was also a centennial celebration of that growing body of theological knowledge called, "Catholic Social Teaching."

Considerable reference is first made to the importance of social justice and the scandals of injustice which were first revealed to the world by *Rerum Novarum.* The first mention of distributive justice particularly, which was made by the former foundational document is highlighted in *Centessimus Annus* section #8:

"The Pope attributed to the "public authority" the "strict duty" of providing properly for the welfare of the workers, because a failure to do so violates justice; indeed, he did not hesitate to speak of "distributive justice (f. 27, RN # 121-123)." It had been clearly seen in the former Social Letter that one portion of citizens, namely the rich and prosperous, cannot be favored, while most citizens are neglected. This is a violation of the law of justice which ordains that every person should receive their due. In any question defending these rights, the defenseless and the poor of society have a claim to special consideration. (CA # 8)

In then moving toward a discussion of "The New Things" of today in Section III of the Letter, John Paul will first discuss the many injustices brought about by the various ideologies and states of the current day, particularly those which had led to the ravages of war. And further, that it is his sincere hope and fervent prayer that people will learn to fight for justice without violence, renouncing class struggle in their internal disputes, and war in international ones. (CA # 22-29)

Distributive justice is an important part of this letter discussed throughout the entirety of section IV. John Paul reaffirms what *Rerum Novarum* and other previous CST Letters have stated in the way of rights to private property and the common purpose of the distribution of material goods. For example, he states this referencing Pope Leo's thoughts on distributive justice from *Rerum Novarum:* " . . . a failure to do so violates justice; indeed, he did not hesitate to speak of 'distributive justice' (CA #8; RN #121-123)"

The universal distribution of goods and their destination must limit the rights to private property as all people in the world should participate in the sharing of these goods. There is a social mortgage on all private property.

"God gave the earth to the whole human race" and has intended the material goods of the earth for all. Distributive justice is discussed further in (CA # 6, 8, 19, 30-43, 57).

It is in Section IV of the Letter, under the heading: PRIVATE PROPERTY AND THE UNIVERSAL DESTINATION OF MATERIAL GOODS, that the subject of distributive justice or the lack of it in society is discussed in a detailed fashion. John Paul first maintains, that regarding the right to property and the common destination of material wealth as it applies to the present time, the question concerning the origin of the material goods which sustain human life, and the satisfaction of people's needs are all an object of their rights. This is because the original source of all that is good is the very act of God. There are many human needs which find no place on the market and because of this, there is a strict duty of justice and truth not to allow fundamental human needs to remain unsatisfied. Further, that society should not allow those burdened by such needs to perish. It is also necessary to help these needy people to acquire expertise, to enter the circle of exchange, and to develop their skills to make the best use of their capacities and resources. Even prior to the logic of a fair exchange of goods and the forms of justice appropriate to it, there exists something which is due to man simply because he is man, and that is due him because of his basic human dignity. Inseparable from that required "something" is the possibility to survive and, at the same time, to make an active contribution to the common good of humanity. (CA # 30-43)

In the light of today's "new things", what needs to be discussed now is the relationship between individual or private property and the universal destination of material wealth. Man reaches his social potential by using both his intelligence and his freedom. In so doing he utilizes the things of this world as objects and instruments and makes them his own.

The foundation of the right to private initiative and ownership is to be found in this activity. By means of his work man commits himself, not only for his own sake but also for others and with others. Each person collaborates in the work of others and for their good. Man works to provide for the needs of his family, his community, his nation, and ultimately all humanity. Moreover, he collaborates in the work of his fellow employees, as well as in the work of suppliers and in the customers' use of goods, in a progressively expanding chain of solidarity. Ownership of the means of production, whether in industry or agriculture, is just and legitimate if it serves useful work. It becomes illegitimate, however, when it is not utilized or when it serves to impede the work of others to gain a profit. This is not the result of the overall expansion of work and the wealth of society, but rather is the result of curbing them or of illicit exploitation, speculation or the breaking of solidarity among working people. Ownership of this kind has no justification, and represents an abuse in the sight of God and man. (CA # 43)

The obligation to earn one's bread by the sweat of one's brow also presumes the right to do so. A society in which this right is systematically denied, in which economic policies do not allow workers to reach satisfactory levels of employment, cannot be justified from an ethical point of view, nor can that society attain social peace." (CA # 43)

It is the love for others, and most particularly a love for the poor, in whom the Church sees Christ himself, which makes concrete, the promotion of justice. Justice will never be fully attained unless people see in the poor person, who is asking for help to survive, not an annoyance or a burden, but an opportunity for showing kindness and a chance for greater enrichment. It is not merely a matter of "giving from one's surplus", but of helping entire peoples which are presently excluded or marginalized. This will empower them and allow them to enter the sphere of economic and human development. "For this to happen, it is not enough to draw on the surplus goods which in fact our world abundantly produces; it requires above all a change of life-styles, of models of production and consumption, and of the established structures of power which today govern societies." (CA # 58)

Regarding her preference for a socio-economic model to present to society, it was stated in the Letter that there were none to present; however, that CST itself might now begin to point the way to develop one. He writes:

> The Church has no models to present; models that are real and truly effective can only arise within the framework of different historical situations, through the efforts of all those who responsibly confront concrete problems in all their social, economic, political and cultural aspects, as these interact with one another. For such a task, the Church offers her social teaching as an indispensable and ideal orientation. (CA # 43)

Chapter Twenty-Three

Distributive Justice in the Social Letters of Pope John Paul II, 1995 and Pope Benedict XVI, 2009

DISTRIBUTIVE JUSTICE IN THE GOSPEL OF LIFE, POPE JOHN PAUL II, 1995

The Gospel of Life, L. *Evangelium Vitae*,[1] was authored by Pope John Paul II in 1995. Life is seen to be a central message of Jesus Christ and the dignity of every human being is stressed from the outset of this Social Letter. Human life is a sharing in the very life of God. (EV # 3)

Mankind should reflect and consider always the violence against life done to millions of human beings, especially children, who are forced into poverty, malnutrition and hunger because of an unjust distribution of resources between nations, peoples, and social classes. What also should be considered is the violence inherent not only in wars, but in the scandalous arms trade, which spawns the many armed conflicts which shed peoples blood and kill life all over the world. This is always being carried on at the expense of the poorest, neediest, and most vulnerable persons in society who are unjustly denied the distribution of food and other resources at the expense of a cadre of weapons purchased. Furthermore, there exists the spreading of death caused by reckless tampering with the world's ecological balance, by the criminal spread of drugs, or by the promotion of certain kinds of sexual activity which, besides being morally unacceptable, also involve grave risks to life. (EV # 10)

Although most of the Gospel of Life Letter pertains to other intense evils in society such as abortion, euthanasia, and capital punishment, there are some very specific statements in John Paul's Letter regarding the violence to life due to a lack of distributive justice. For example:

> How can we fail to consider the violence against life done to millions of human beings, especially children, who are forced into poverty, malnutrition and hunger because of an unjust distribution of resources between peoples and between social classes (EV # 10)?

And:

> They must then make efforts to ensure greater opportunities and a fairer distribution of wealth so that everyone can share equitably in the goods of creation. Solutions must be sought on the global level by establishing a true economy of communion and sharing of goods, in both the national and international order (EV # 91).

An important part of policies which speak in favor of life is the issue of population growth. Public authorities have a responsibility to "intervene to orient the demography of the population". But such interventions must always respect the primary and inalienable responsibility of married couples and families. Methods should never be employed which fail to respect the person and fundamental human rights, beginning with the right to life of every innocent human being. Therefore, it is morally unacceptable to encourage or impose, the use of methods such as contraception, sterilization and abortion to regulate births. The ways of solving the population problem are quite different. Governments and the various international agencies must above all strive to create economic, social, public health and cultural conditions which will enable married couples to make their choices about procreation in full freedom and with genuine responsibility. They must then make efforts to ensure "greater opportunities and a fairer distribution of wealth so that everyone can share equitably in the goods of creation." Solutions must be sought on the global level by establishing a true economy of communion and sharing of goods, in both the national and international order. This is the only way to respect the dignity of persons and families. Without a fair and equitable distribution of goods and resources-anti-birth policies will continue to be enacted. (EV # 91)

The Gospel of Life is for the whole of human society. "To be actively pro-life is to contribute to the renewal of society through the promotion of the common good (EV # 101)."

DISTRIBUTIVE JUSTICE IN CHARITY IN TRUTH, POPE BENEDICT XVI, 2009

Charity in Truth, L. *Caritas in Veritate*,[2] was the only Social Letter authored by Pope Benedict XVI in 2009 upon the death of the much beloved John Paul II. First, Benedict compares charity and justice by stating that: "every society draws up its own system of justice." But, charity goes beyond justice, because to love is to give, to offer what belongs to me to the other. However, charity never lacks justice, because it asks us to give to the other what is rightfully his. We give to him what is his due, because of his being or his acting. Justice is inseparable from charity. However, charity transcends justice. One must desire the common good and strive toward it as a requirement of justice and charity. The more we strive to secure the common good by meeting our neighbor's needs, the more we demonstrate that we love them. Today, there is an urgent need for reform in society due to great and growing injustices in the development of peoples. This urgency is a consequence of "Charity in Truth." (CV # 6)

From the social point of view, systems of protection and welfare, already present in many countries, are finding it hard to pursue their goals of true distributive justice in today's profoundly changed environment. Indeed, they could find it even harder in the future. This is because: "The global market has stimulated first and foremost, on the part of rich countries, a search for areas in which to outsource production at low cost with a view to reducing the prices of many goods (CV # 25)."

The basic human dignity of each individual and the demands of distributive justice require today, that economic choices do not cause disparities in wealth to increase in both an excessive and morally unacceptable manner. Furthermore, we must continue to prioritize the goal of access to steady employment for everyone. Through the systemic increase of social inequality, situations of dire poverty have continued to be created and to grow. This has not been the case just within any single country, but between the populations of several different countries. (CV # 32) In a climate of mutual trust, in any encounter between persons, the market is the economic institution that permits this encounter. Contracts regulate their relations in these encounters as they exchange goods and services of equivalent value between them. The market is subject to the principles of commutative justice, which regulates the relations of giving and receiving between parties to a transaction. This is provided only when members are all treated equally under the law. But, in the doctrine of the Church, CST has unceasingly highlighted the importance of distributive justice and social justice for the market economy. (CV # 35-39)

In fact, if the market is governed solely by the principle of value equivalency in the exchange of goods, it cannot produce the social cohesion that it requires to function well. There must exist internal forms of solidarity and mutual trust in these encounters, without which the market cannot completely carry out its proper economic function. In society today, it is this trust which has ceased to exist, and the absence of trust has left a big vacuum. The market cannot simply rely on itself, because it is not able to produce by itself alone something that lies outside its competence. Economic activity, to solve social problems, needs to be directed towards the interests of the common good. Unless this is the case, grave imbalances will be produced. This occurs when economic action, conceived merely as an engine for wealth creation, is detached from political action which is conceived as a means for pursuing justice through redistribution in the pursuit of the common good. (CV # 36)

Throughout Section Three of the Letter, there is a very clear call for increased distributive justice in society to demonstrate the living message of charity in truth. For example:

> The social doctrine of the Church has unceasingly highlighted the importance of distributive justice and social justice for the market economy, not only because it belongs within a broader social and political context, but also because of the wider network of relations within which it operates (CV #35).

> It must be borne in mind that grave imbalances are produced when economic action, conceived merely as an engine for wealth creation, is detached from political action, conceived as a means for pursuing justice through redistribution (CV #36).

And:

> The Church's social doctrine has always maintained that justice must be applied to every phase of economic activity, because this is always concerned with man and his needs...all the other phases in the economic cycle inevitably have moral implications. Thus, every economic decision has a moral consequence...Economic life undoubtedly requires contracts to regulate relations of exchange between goods of equivalent value. But it also needs just laws and forms of redistribution governed by politics (CV #37).

Also:

> Paul VI, in *Populorum Progressio,* called for the creation of a model of market economy capable of including within its range all peoples and not just the better off. He called for efforts to build a more human world for all, a world in which "all will be able to give and receive, without one group making progress at the expense of the other." In this way, he was applying on a global scale the insights and aspirations contained in *Rerum Novarum,*[3] written at a time during the Industrial Revolution, when the idea was first proposed — somewhat ahead of its time — that the civil order, for its self-regulation, also needed intervention from the State for purposes of redistribution (CV #39).

And finally:

> The processes of globalization, suitably understood and directed, open up the unprecedented possibility of large-scale redistribution of wealth on a world-wide scale; if badly directed, however, they can lead to an increase in poverty and inequality, and could even trigger a global crisis. It is necessary to correct the malfunctions, some of them serious, that cause new divisions between peoples and within peoples, and to ensure that the redistribution of wealth does not come about through the redistribution or increase of poverty (CV # 42).

CST has always maintained that justice must be applied to every phase of economic activity, because economic activity must always consider the basic human dignity of man and his needs. At one time, it may have been conceivable that first the creation of wealth could be entrusted to the economy, and then the task of distributing it in a just manner could be assigned to the political realm. Today that would be virtually impossible because economic activity is no longer contained or carried out within just the confines of territorial limits, but is global, while the political authority of governments continues to be principally localized and is not universal. "Consequently, social and distributive justice must be a consideration from the outset, as the economic process unfolds. It cannot be a consideration when the economic process concludes or an incidental consequence of it (CV # 37)."

The economy needs ethics for it to function properly, and not just any generic kind of ethics, but an ethics which is people-centered. Economic and ethical decisions and choices should never be allowed to stand which will end up being contrary to social justice and true human welfare and concern. "Today, while unprecedented injustices seem to be widely tolerated around the world, the desperate poor and needy of the world continue to knock on the doors of the rich. But, the wealthy nations of the world now run the risk of no longer hearing those knocks, due to developing consciences that can no longer distinguish what is intrinsically human." (CV # 45-48, 75)

This implies that the economy, by its very nature, must first listen and hear the knocking to be considered in any way, as ethically inspired.

In his Conclusion, Pope Benedict tells us:

> Without God man neither knows which way to go, nor even understands who he is...Only a humanism open to the Absolute can guide us in the promotion and building of forms of social and civic life — structures, institutions, culture and ethos...*Caritas in Veritate*, from which authentic development proceeds, is not produced by us, but given to us (CV # 78-79).

Chapter Twenty-Four

Distributive Justice in the Social Letters of Pope Francis

DISTRIBUTIVE JUSTICE IN THE JOY OF THE GOSPEL

The Joy of the Gospel, L. *Evangelii Gaudium,*[1] was authored by our current Holy Father, Pope Francis, in the year 2013. Francis, from the beginning of this Letter, will address the problem of distributive injustice in society. He sees today's world as being pervaded by consumerism. This, he feels is: "The desolation and anguish born of a complacent yet covetous heart, the feverish pursuit of frivolous pleasures, and a blunted conscience." Whenever and wherever human persons are caught up in their own interests and self-concerns, this will have as its result, "no room for others, no place for the poor." We should be scandalized because we know that there is enough food for everyone on the planet and that hunger is the result of a poor distribution of goods and income. The problem is made worse because consumerism fosters what can only be called "a generalized practice of wastefulness." Today's economic mechanisms promote a society of conspicuous consumption, yet it is evident that the combination of unbridled consumerism and inequality proves doubly damaging to the social fabric. (EG # 2,60)

Human beings are today considered as consumer goods themselves, to be used and then discarded. We have created a "throw away" culture which is now growing. "It is no longer simply about exploitation and oppression, but something new. Exclusion, ultimately means not being a part of the society in which we live; those excluded are no longer society's underside or its fringes or its disenfranchised – they are no longer even a part of it. The excluded are not the "exploited" but the outcast, the "leftovers." (EG # 53-54)

He speaks of a developing "globalization of indifference." Today, some people continue to defend existing outdated trickle-down theories which assume that economic growth, encouraged by a free market, will inevitably succeed in bringing about greater justice and inclusiveness in the world. This has at its core, a naïve trust in the goodness of those wielding economic power. Meanwhile, the desperate poor and needy are excluded from the prevailing economic system while a few maintain a lifestyle which excludes most of the people in the world. (EG # 54)

"The distribution of wealth, concern for the poor, and human rights cannot be suppressed under the guise of creating a consensus on paper or a transient peace for a contented minority." The existing socio-economic system is simply unjust at its root, and just as goodness tends to spread, the toleration of evil, which is injustice, tends to expand its creeping influence in society and the economy. (EG # 218)

The Church is called to be the house of the Father, with doors always wide open and a mother with an open heart. As in previous Encyclicals, we are exhorted to an "ever watchful scrutiny of the signs of the times." Then Francis proceeds to talk about an economy of exclusion and inequality where a globalization of indifference has developed. Trickle-down theories which assume that economic growth, encouraged by a free market, will inevitably succeed in bringing about greater justice and inclusiveness in the world, have failed to produce.

Today's economic mechanisms promote inordinate consumption, yet it is evident that unbridled consumerism combined with inequality proves doubly damaging to the social fabric. Money has become an idol. The thirst for power and possessions knows no limits. Behind this attitude lurks a rejection of ethics and a rejection of God. What is called for is an evangelization capable of shedding light on these new ways of relating to God, to others and to the world around us, and inspiring essential values. . .The Joy of the Gospel is such that it cannot be taken away from us by anyone or anything (cf. Jn. 16:22).[2] The evils of our world – and those of the Church – must not be excuses for diminishing our commitment and our fervor. We should be realists, but without losing our joy, our boldness, and our hope-filled commitment. Let us not allow ourselves to be robbed of missionary vigor (EG #46-109)!

Francis then turns his attention to "The Social Dimension of Evangelization" because the task of evangelization implies and demands the integral promotion of each human being. In this section, much will be said concerning the preferential option for the poor and a lack of distributive justice in society. Here are many examples:

> Solidarity is a spontaneous reaction by those who recognize that the social function of property and the universal destination of goods are realities which

> come before private property. The private ownership of goods is justified by the need to protect and increase them, so that they can better serve the common good; for this reason, solidarity must be lived as the decision to restore to the poor what belongs to them (EG #189).

And:

> In all places and circumstances, Christians, with the help of their pastors, are called to hear the cry of the poor...Seeing their poverty, hearing their cries and knowing their sufferings, we are scandalized because we know that there is enough food for everyone and that hunger is the result of a poor distribution of goods and income (EG #191).

Also:

> The dignity of each human person and the pursuit of the common good are concerns which ought to shape all economic policies...How many words prove irksome to this system! It is irksome when the question of ethics is raised, when global solidarity is invoked, when the distribution of goods is mentioned, when reference is made to protecting labor and defending the dignity of the powerless, when allusion is made to a God who demands a commitment to justice (EG#203).
>
> ***
>
> "We can no longer trust in the unseen forces and the invisible hand of the market. Growth in justice requires more than economic growth...it requires decisions, programs, mechanisms and processes specifically geared to a better distribution of income, the creation of sources of employment and an integral promotion of the poor which goes beyond a simple welfare mentality (EG #204)."

And finally:

> Demands involving the distribution of wealth, concern for the poor and human rights cannot be suppressed under the guise of creating a consensus on paper or a transient peace for a contented minority. The dignity of the human person and the common good should rank higher than the comfort of those who refuse to renounce their privileges. When these values are threatened, a prophetic voice must be raised (EG #218).

We cannot simply trust in the unseen forces and the invisible hand of the market anymore. Justice requires more than economic growth, while presupposing such growth: it requires: "decisions, programs, mechanisms and processes specifically geared to a better distribution of income, the creation of sources of employment and an integral promotion of the poor which goes beyond a simple welfare mentality." The economy can no longer try to remedy the situation through attempting to increase profits by reducing the existing work force and by doing this, add to the ranks of the excluded. The human dignity of every person and the pursuit of the common good are two primary concerns which ought to shape all economic policies. (EG # 204, 241)

Toward the end of the Letter, Francis will discuss solidarity, the social function of property, and the universal destination of goods. He views these as realities which must come before the ownership of private property. "The private ownership of goods is justified by the need to protect and increase them, so that they can better serve the common good; for this reason, solidarity must be lived as the decision to restore to the poor what belongs to them." What is being said, essentially is, that private property always has a social mortgage. (EG # 189) One of the answers that Francis sees to address the many problems brought about by creeping social and distributive injustice in the world is a true evangelizing zeal in the hearts of the many followers of Christ.

He then proclaims to us what he believes to be the only answer:

"After having considered some of the challenges of the present, I would now like to speak of the task which bears upon us in every age and place, for "there can be no true evangelization without the explicit proclamation of Jesus as Lord", and without "the primacy of the proclamation of Jesus Christ in all evangelizing work." (EG # 110-175)

DISTRIBUTIVE JUSTICE IN PRAISE BE: ON CARE FOR OUR COMMON HOME

Praise Be: On Care for our Common Home, L. *Laudato Si,*[3] is the latest and most recent Social Letter authored by Pope Francis in 2015. The Letter makes a major connection between distributive justice and the environment for the first time. It also makes several connections between an economy of conspicuous consumption and a lack of distributive justice. Francis initially makes note that there are ethical and spiritual roots to the world's environmental problems. (LS # 9)

The Letter indicates that climate change, being a world-wide problem, has a host of grave implications which affect environmental, social, economic, and political issues as well as creating many severe injustices concerning the distribution of goods. It represents one of the principal obstacles facing humankind in our day. Its worst impact will probably be felt by the developing countries in years to come. Global warming, often caused by huge consumption on the part of some rich countries, has repercussions on the poorest areas of the world. Most of the planet's poor often live in areas particularly affected by phenomena related to warming. Their means of subsistence is largely dependent on natural reserves and eco-systemic services such as agriculture, fishing and forestry. They have no other financial activities or resources which can enable them to adapt to climate change or face natural disasters. This is not to mention the fact that their access to social services and protection is very limited. For example, changes in climate, to which animals and plants cannot adapt, lead them to migrate; this in turn affects the livelihood of the poor, who are then forced to leave their homes and migrate themselves. Sadly, there is widespread indifference to their cries of suffering. Our lack of response to these cries of suffering and tragedies which involves our neighbors, gives rise to a loss of that sense of responsibility for our fellow men and women upon which all civil society is founded. (LS # 25)

Those who live in wealthier countries who possess most of the key resources and economic or political power seem mostly concerned with covering up the many problems or concealing their symptoms. They simply make little or no effort to reduce the disease brought on by the negative impacts of climate change. However, many of these multiple symptoms seem to indicate that such effects will continue to worsen if we simply continue with the current models of production and consumption. The planet has enough natural resources to supply all our needs, however, it cannot continue to sustain all our wants and desires. The rapid depletion of natural resources cannot continue to sustain the present level of consumption in developed countries and wealthier sectors of society. There, the habit of wasting and discarding of goods has reached unprecedented levels. This exploitation of the planet and conspicuous consumption has already exceeded acceptable limits and we are still nowhere near the point of starting to find solutions to solve the problems of the poor, needy, and most vulnerable. If we are listening, we will hear both the cry of the earth and the cry of the poor simultaneously. (LS # 27-31)

Caring for the environment demands vision and far-sightedness. No one looking for quick and easy profit is truly interested in reflecting on this. But the cost of the damage caused by such selfish lack of concern is much greater than the economic benefits to be obtained. Many believe that we can simply stand by and be silent witnesses to a multitude of these terrible social injustices. But, this is only the case if we think that we can obtain significant economic benefits by making the rest of humanity, present and future, pay the extremely high costs of environmental deterioration. We forget, however, that the rest of humanity includes our children and our children's children. (LS # 3, 36, 43, 56, 109)

Some wish to indicate that a reduction in the birth rate would be a means of solving many of the world's problems. But to blame population growth instead of extreme and selective consumerism on the part of some, is one way of refusing to face the issues. It is an attempt to legitimize the present model of distribution, where a minority believes that it has the right to conspicuously consume in a way which can never be universalized. The planet could not even contain the waste products of such consumption. Approximately, one-third of all food produced is discarded, and "whenever food is thrown out it is as if it were stolen from the table of the poor." (LS # 50-52)

The prevailing economy accepts every advance in technology with a view to profit, without concern for its potentially negative impact on human beings. Finance overwhelms the real economy. Some people even maintain that current economics and technology will solve all environmental problems eventually. They argue that the problems of global hunger and poverty will eventually be resolved simply by market growth. They show no interest in distributive justice through more balanced levels of production, a better distribution of wealth, concern for the environment, and the rights of future generations. For them, maximizing profits is enough. But, the environment is one of those goods that cannot be adequately safeguarded or promoted by market forces. We need to reject a pie in the sky conception of the market, which suggests that problems can be solved simply by an increase in the profits of companies or individuals. And the marketplace, in and of itself, cannot ever guarantee that there will be human development, social inclusion, and distributive justice for the many. People are people and the marketplace is a thing. CST from its outset has always proclaimed, "people before things." (LS # 109)

The earth is essentially a shared inheritance, whose fruits are meant to benefit everyone. Because the world was created for everyone, every ecological approach needs to incorporate a social perspective. This should always include the fundamental rights of the poor and the underprivileged. The principle of the subordination of private property to the universal destination of goods, and thus the right of everyone to their use, is a golden rule of social conduct and the first principle of the whole ethical and social order. "The Christian tradition has never recognized the right to private property as absolute or inviolable, and has stressed the social purpose of all forms of private property." (LS # 93)

In several of his recent previous Social Letters, Pope John Paul II has also stated that:

> The Church does indeed defend the legitimate right to private property, but she also teaches no less clearly that there is always a social mortgage on all private property, in order that goods may serve the general purpose that God gave them…it is not in accord with God's plan that this gift be used in such a way that its benefits favor only a few[4]

An integral ecology cannot be separated from the notion of the common good. This is a central and unifying principle of social ethics. The common good is "the sum of those conditions of social life which allow social groups and their individual members relatively thorough and ready access to their own fulfilment." Underlying the principle of the common good is respect for the human person. It has also to do with the overall welfare of society and the development of a variety of intermediate groups, applying the Principle of Subsidiarity. Outstanding among those groups is the family, "the domestic church," as the basic cell of all society.

In a section on "Global Inequality," Francis will discuss distributive justice and the lack of it in society at great length. He believes that the human environment and the natural environment deteriorate together. He will take up the issue of a lack of distributive Justice not only here, but in several other parts of this Letter as well. Here are some examples:

> Climate change is a global problem with grave implications: environmental, social, economic, political, and for the distribution of goods (LS #25).

And:

> To blame population growth instead of extreme and selective consumerism by some is one way of refusing to face the issues. It is an attempt to legitimize the present model of distribution, where a minority believes that it has the right to consume in a way which can never be universalized (LS #50).
>
> ***
>
> The principle of the subordination of private property to the universal destination of goods, and thus the right of everyone to their use, is a golden rule of social conduct and 'the first principle of the whole ethical and social order'...the Church does indeed defend the legitimate right to private property, but she also teaches no less clearly that there is always a social mortgage on all private property, in order that goods may serve the general purpose that God gave them (LS #93)."

Also:

> They are less concerned with certain economic theories which today scarcely anybody dares defend, than with their actual operation in the functioning of the economy. They may not affirm such theories with words, but nonetheless support them with their deeds by showing no interest in more balanced levels of production, a better distribution of wealth, concern for the environment and the rights of future generations. Their behavior shows that for them maximizing profits is enough (LS#109).

And finally:

> The common good calls for social peace, the stability and security provided by a certain order which cannot be achieved without concern particularly for distributive justice; whenever this is violated, violence always ensues (LS #157)." Today in society, injustices abound and growing numbers of people are deprived of their basic human rights and are simply considered expendable. "The principle of the common good immediately becomes a summons to

> solidarity and to make a "preferential option for the poor." This option entails recognizing the implications of the universal destination of the world's goods, but it also demands, before all else, an appreciation of the immense dignity of the poor. (LS # 156-158).

Distributive justice in the world will only come about if there is a profound change of humanity. It requires that we, especially those of us in wealthier countries, who profess to be Christian, replace consumption with sacrifice, greed with generosity, wastefulness with a spirit of sharing. It also requires us to embrace an asceticism which entails learning to give, and not simply to give up. As Francis tells us, in this, his most recent Social Letter:

> It is a way of loving, of moving gradually away from what I want and desire to what God's world needs. It is liberation from fear, greed and compulsion. As Christians, we are also called to accept the world as a sacrament of communion, as a way of sharing with God and our neighbors on a global scale. It is our humble conviction that the divine and the human meet in the slightest detail in the seamless garment of God's creation, in the last speck of dust of our planet (LS # 9).

At the very center of our being human, this is where we meet the divine and through faith we believe that we are not just dust; we are "beloved dust."

Chapter Twenty-Five

From Distributive Justice to Distributism

G.K. CHESTERTON AND HILAIRE BELLOC

Pope Leo's Social Letter, *Rerum Novarum,* written in 1891[1], was the foundational launch of CST, and as mentioned, it had much to say about distributive justice. However, the intention of the Letter was not to launch a new economic system, but merely to highlight the problems which existed in Modern Capitalism and to attempt to halt the onslaught of Socialism as a response to Laissez Faire Capitalism. The Pope's Letter did provide the basis however, for the recognized founders of the economic theory of Distributism, G.K. Chesterton, English Catholic writer and theologian, and writer and historian Hilaire Belloc, to propose the new theory.[2] They expanded the thought of CST on distributive justice by articulating a newly proposed economic theory. Their economic theory was totally and radically at odds with not only Socialism and Communism, but Capitalism as well. The functioning of this new economic system was not to be dependent on the state as was the case with Socialism and Communism, nor was it to be dependent on the individual as conspicuous consumer as was the case with Capitalism; Distributism would depend on the family in communal solidarity as the heart of its ability to function.

Gilbert Keith Chesterton's and Hilaire Belloc's initial premise was very simple; it was that private property should be divided into the smallest possible freeholds and then be distributed justly across society. In other words, the distribution of "property" would be according to what was "proper." The motivation for their thinking stemmed from a basic belief that big government and big business were "in cahoots" with each other and not working to benefit the common man. They had a deep distrust for all concentrations of wealth and power. The heart of this economic distribution theory, however, had more to do with the distribution of power than it did with the distribution of wealth. The wealth and other resources would flow from the distribution of power. In society, the Catholic Principle of Subsidiarity would naturally allow for this. In his writings, Chesterton was greatly influenced by the Catholic theology of Thomas Aquinas who formalized the Principle of Subsidiarity based on the philosophy of Aristotle. Aquinas had developed the idea that societies naturally progress from families (T.A. *Summa* I-II, Q. 106).[3] Therefore, decisions should be made at a local level whenever possible, rather than by a central authority, such as the state, with complete authoritative power. Because their economic theory proposed a wider distribution of capital in society, this thinking could also be summed up with one of Chesterton's favorite quotes:

> "It is not that there are too many capitalists, it's that there are too few."[4]

To go from a Capitalist economic model of society to a Distributist economic model is not simple or easy, but it can be done. The movement must begin from the bottom up as a groundswell and not the top down. It cannot be forced onto society and must start with the will of the people who truly seek distributive justice in society.

At the heart of the movement is a love for God and neighbor which initiates a desire for change. And then it develops with people who view the human dignity and well-being of every person as contributing to the overall common good. Chesterton believed that we generally seek out after happiness but often pursue pleasure in the mistaken understanding that it is the same thing as happiness. He saw ethics as a safeguard against economic greed and selfishness. He also saw the home and the family as being a cornerstone of socio-economic life. After all, even the word "economics," had evolved from the Greek word *oikos* which meant "household."[5] We had gone far afield of that in society and needed to return home. Both Chesterton and Belloc, believing strongly in the Catholic Principle of Subsidiarity, maintained that government should be as small as possible and only as big as necessary. Politics should be kept to the local level whenever possible. Another one of Chesterton's favorite quotes regarding Distributism was:

> "What we should try to do is make politics as local as possible; keep the politicians near enough to kick them."[6]

All of Chesterton's writings on Distributism were woven with a style he personally developed and threaded throughout all his Catholic thinking and writing. He delighted in the art of using paradox, hyperbole, allegory, humor and irony, aphorisms, oxymoron, mutually exclusive extremes and opposites, as well as stark contrasts and contradictions. He saw this through a Chesterton lens which brought vividness and imagination, not only to describing and animating poetically his economic theory of Distributism, but even more generally in his writing about all Catholic Christianity. In one of his best-known works, *Orthodoxy,* Chesterton writes on the paradoxes of Christianity:

> It is true that the historic Church has at once emphasized celibacy and emphasized the family…It has kept them side by side like two strong colors, red and white, like the red and white upon the shield of St. George. It has always had a healthy hatred of pink. It hates that combination of two colors…It hates that evolution of black into white which is tantamount to a dirty gray (*Orthodoxy*; G.K.C., p.11).[7]

This paradox could also be seen and perhaps summed up in another favorite quote of Chesterton's:

> "There is nothing queerer today than the importance of unimportant things; except, of course, the unimportance of important things."[8]

Chesterton viewed God as the "God of surprises." In many ways, he was like a little child taking delight in saying, "Do it again daddy," as the Lord did seemingly ordinary feats like making the sun rise each morning. He was awed by the stark contrasts and paradoxes of Christianity, depicted in things like the mighty God becoming a little baby, the incarnation, the crucifixion and resurrection, the tender mercy and intense anger of Jesus, graced nature, God's immanence and transcendence, seeing the unseen, the Kingdom in our midst and yet to come, lions lying with lambs, dying into new life, becoming foolish to be wise, sorrow becoming joy, the last being first, family and celibacy, etc. He carried these contradictions and paradoxes into his writings on Distributism and in many ways, he captured all this with his own brand of "serious playfulness."

In writing on Distributism and Capitalism in The *Outline of Sanity*, Chesterton writes:

> Capitalism is contradictory as soon as it is complete; because it is dealing with the mass of men in two different ways at once. When most men are wage earners, it is more and more difficult for most men to be customers. For the capitalist is always trying to cut down what his servant demands, and in doing so is cutting down what his customer can spend…He is wanting the same man to be rich and poor at the same time (*Outline of Sanity*, G.K.C.).[9]

In continually stressing the importance of distributive justice in society and economics, none of the modern Popes who authored the aforementioned Social Letters ever intended to propose a new economic theory, such as

Distributism. They merely sought to be advocates for distributive justice and continually called on those in leadership roles in society to correct the many distributive injustices inherent in the systems and institutions of their day.

When Chesterton and Belloc proposed their new economic theory, they only had the two Social Letters of Pope Leo XIII and Pius XI to draw from which were written in 1891 and 1931 respectively.[10] The body of theology formalized over the next 100+ years, which is today called "Catholic Social Teaching," was not available to them. Today, we can discuss the economic theory of Distributism and know first what Chesterton and Belloc had to say about it. But, we now have additionally what all the many Holy Fathers in their Social Letters had to say about distributive justice after the time these two individuals lived and died. Furthermore, we also have the benefit of 20-20 hindsight in looking at the historical successes and failures in the evolution of the three major economic systems of modern times, Capitalism, Socialism, and Communism. It allows us to measure Distributism not only against the failed Socialism and Communism experiments, but also against the prevailing economic system of unrestrained and unfettered "Real Capitalism," as opposed to the economic theory of "Idealist Capitalism."

Chapter Twenty-Six

Distributism-Toward a New Economy

Since Chesterton's death in 1936, many thought that Distributism as an economic theory would die as well. Though many tried to bury it with him, it continues to rise like a Phoenix and come to life as other economic systems begin to unravel or show that they evolve very differently in reality and practice than they existed as idealized economic theories.

At this moment in time, Distributism, because it is still untested and untried, is no more than a collective dream about a socio-economic system that is based on the principle of distributive justice. The importance and value of distributive justice in all socio-economic decisions has been emphasized by the 7 popes who wrote the 13 Catholic Social Encyclicals over the previous century.[1] The Second Vatican Council also stressed its importance to society.[2] So, its foundation is solid, with its roots first in the Bible and Judeo-Christian Tradition and then built on the Social Teaching of the Catholic Church, based on what has heretofore been outlined previously concerning distributive justice.

As we have stated earlier in Section Two, the first Catholic Social Letter in 1891, *Rerum Novarum* had this to say concerning distributive justice:

> Among the many and grave duties of rulers who would do their best for the people, the first and chief is to act with strict justice—with that justice which is called distributive—toward each and every class alike (RN#33).[3]

Most every Catholic Social Letter written by the modern Popes since 1981, up to and including Pope Francis today, has had much to say about the ongoing lack of distributive justice in society and in the world's economic systems, structures, and institutions. They have condemned both Communist and Socialist systems outright and severely criticized laissez faire Capitalism as being "unfettered, unrestrained, and even scandalous." In hindsight, The

Capitalist system can be viewed today as blended with the conspicuous consumption of a consumerist society and the deification of the marketplace at the expense of the human dignity of persons.

Capitalism, in its evolution, has historically reshaped the worldwide economic landscape through globalization, free trade, property rights, entrepreneurship, and the spread of the rule of law. However, the control of capital and power has also historically evolved into fewer and fewer wealthy hands and reshaped the concept of Idealist Capitalism itself. In doing so, it has diminished human dignity, created increasing inequality among people, and has nurtured an almost complete disregard for the principal of distributive justice. The billions spent on anti-poverty programs since the advent of Capitalism has made poverty and inequality more bearable, but it certainly hasn't made it any more escapable for many of the people affected by it.

In *The Outline of Sanity*, making the case for Distributism, Chesterton argued:

> They say it is Utopian; and they are right. They say it is idealistic; and they are right. They say it is quixotic; and they are right. It deserves every name that will indicate how completely they have driven justice out of the world . . .[4]

Distributism as an economic system is fully compliant with all the principles of every Papal Social Letter, particularly on the protection of human dignity and the flourishing of social justice in society. As a system, at its heart it believes in loving God and neighbor and in Gospel values. It is focused on the home and family and centered on the widest possible ownership of property as the best guarantee of political and economic freedom. It seeks to move away from being a system where the concentration of ownership is in the hands of a few wealthy capitalists or even worse, the state. Consonant with CST, it places persons before things like systems, structures, and institutions.

There is a major difference between Utopian Capitalism and Real Capitalism. Today, Capitalism is not based simply on the right to private property and competition in a free market system, which is what many people still believe it to be. In today's Capitalist system, the wealth in the system is controlled by a very select few rather than the many. For the most part, the ownership of capital is separated from the work on that capital and the laws in place facilitate that separation to the advantage of the very wealthy few. This has become extreme in its lopsidedness to the point where a recent Oxfam America report showed that the world's 8 richest individuals hold more wealth than the 3.6 billion poorest people, about half the world's population. Furthermore, in the United States, the top 10% of the population controls 90% of the wealth.[5]

CST has many themes which were discussed in the first part of this book, but one of the foremost is the dignity of the human person in the eyes of God. The dignity of the human person should be the measure of any modern economic system. In modern Capitalism, markets should be structured to reflect that reality, but the reality is that markets are far more important to the system than the people they should be serving. And the market alone can never produce a just distribution of wealth and power. This is because the controlling hands of the wealthy and powerful capitalist will always be at work greedily grabbing the available capital with one hand, while not releasing its grip on the markets with the other hand. Sadly, what we have seen in the evolution of Capitalism is a deification of the holy marketplace.

One should never expect any economic system which is based on the rule of law to ultimately make society virtuous. However, we can and should expect our economic system to distribute the wealth, power, and resources contained in it justly, broadly, and equitably. What we find in modern Capitalism is that the marketplace, labor-owner friction, the stock markets, the concentration of wealth, the perpetuation of monopolies, powerful conglomerates, the centrality of consumerism, GDP, and the favoritism found in unjust laws to benefit big business, are all far more important than the people the Capitalist economy is intended to serve. Today's Capitalist system, by its own design, simply places the importance of things before persons, families, or the common good. The opposite is true with the economic theory of Distributism.

With all that having been said, perhaps one of its remaining positives, is that the current system of Real Capitalism remains preferable to both state run Socialism and Communism which have proven to be even worse and utter and total failures. However, as it exists today, it is not working for the common good of most of the people in the system. Though we may rightly call Real Capitalism an imperfect system, we must always keep in mind that currently it is our finest form of imperfection until a better economic system comes along and is nurtured and developed to eventually replace it.

Pope Francis has labelled the modern Capitalist system, "scandalous." And he has said in his modern Social Letter, "*The Joy of the Gospel*":

> . . . today we also have to say "thou shalt not" to an economy of exclusion and inequality. Such an economy kills. How can it be that it is not a news item when an elderly homeless person dies of exposure, but it is news when the stock market loses two points? This is a case of exclusion (EG #53).

And more recently in his Social Letter, *Praise Be:*

> The economy accepts every advance in technology with a view to profit, without concern for its potentially negative impact on human beings . . . Finally, the common good calls for social peace, the stability and security

> provided by a certain order which cannot be achieved without particular concern for distributive justice (LS # 109, 157).

This is not to say that everyone who uses the modern Capitalist system to their advantage today is a tyrant or is unethical. There are many ethical people who profit from the economics of the Capitalist system even though some might say, as Gordon Gekko did in the movie "*Wall St.*", "Greed is good."[6] Most of these people believe that ethics is just simply "good business" in any economic decision. But, this is far from the issue at hand because they would probably also say that even though ethical decisions are beneficial for business, ethics should not be considered or play any defining role in shaping any modern scientific economic theory.

However, ethics is not a part of economics; economics is a part of the study of the field of ethics. The justification for this has been confirmed in many of the Social Letters of the modern Popes. This is particularly evident in several of the more recent Social Letters of Pope Benedict XVI, Pope John Paul II, and Pope Francis such as *Charity in Truth*, *On the Social Concern of the Church, The One Hundredth Year, and Joy of the Gospel.*[7]

Ethics, as a dimension of Moral Theology has to do with the interactions between people and thus economics which also concerns itself with those interactions becomes a part of the study of the field of ethics.

This is something that will always be at the heart of what has gone wrong with Real Capitalism. Unlike Distributism, where wealth and power is spread broadly across the entire system, in Capitalism, wealth and power are in the hands of the few and not the many. Furthermore, the philosophy behind Capitalism is a utilitarian as opposed to a humanitarian view of life as is the case in Distributism. This allows persons to separate economics from ethics. This will always have injustice as the end result, because the modern Capitalist will understand the word "distributive" to only mean "supplying goods to stores and other businesses that sell to consumers." They will be blind therefore, to distributive justice, always missing the true connection between the two words. They will not see the connection between the word "distributive" and the word "justice" which makes it both a socio-economic, and primarily an ethical term.

Consistent with CST, Distributism seeks to subordinate economic activity to human life holistically. It becomes not only part of humanity's economic life, but our spiritual, social, political, and family life as well. A central difference in Distributism is in the organizing principle of society. Unlike Capitalism, where the basic organizing principle is the individual, who by himself or herself, apart from a group, cannot be in a relationship and constitute a society, or Socialism where the basic organizing principle is the state; in Distributism, the basic organizing principle is the family. This has been a dimension of Catholic thought since the time of Thomas Aquinas.[8]

At the heart of Distributism is the family unit. The family is the central and primary functioning socio-economic unit within society with an aim for the common good of all in society. Families, in community, address common things which one single family might not be able to accomplish on its own. Any levels of government only come in to play as communities are unable to address and accomplish certain things on their own. Government involvement must start at the local level. The Catholic Principle of Subsidiarity would always apply here. It is a bottom-up and not top-down approach to the organization of society.

Regarding the environment, because distributive justice is seen to be both an economic as well as an ethical term, Distributists would often be naturally sensitive to environmental issues. There would be recognition that environmental issues affect the poorest, weakest, and most vulnerable in society first and this ultimately affects the common good. Distributists would view the environment as God's creation, therefore there would naturally be respect for the earth. There would also be recognition that the earth produces enough resources to meet all our needs, it just doesn't produce enough to meet all our wants. Consuming less means saving the earth's resources not only for ourselves, but for our children, who in coming generations will live and work in the families of the future. Unlike Capitalism, Distributism is not dependent on increasing levels of consumerism for its perpetuation.

Conspicuous consumption is a term which was introduced by the Norwegian-American economist Thorstein Veblen in his book, *The Theory of the Leisure Class*. The book was published in 1899, shortly after Pope Leo XIII authored his foundational document of CST, *Rerum Novarum* in 1891.[9] The term, conspicuous consumption, refers to rabid-like consumers who buy expensive items to display and flaunt their wealth and income rather than to use those products for their practical utility. The result of this, according to Veblen, is a society characterized by waste; wasted time, wasted money, and particularly wasted goods and resources. The term, conspicuous consumption, was originally used to depict the upper class that formed in the 19th century because of the Second Industrial Revolution. But, it is certainly applicable to most of Capitalist society today which is characterized by addictive and narcissistic behavior influenced by consumerism as an integral part of the functioning of the modern society.

As an outgrowth of conspicuous consumption, a marketing technique known as "perceived obsolescence," was developed by corporate America as businesses began to introduce new products in rapid succession which are supposedly better, smarter, faster, or a step up from those products which had been launched previously. The psychological effects make it appear that the consumer must have this newer product or they will continue to own a product which is certainly functioning and useful, but obsolete, out of date, old-fashioned, or lacks style. The automobile and clothing manufacturers were on the leading edge of this new technique as a new model or a new line was and still is introduced every year, but the cell phone companies have taken this to a fine consumer artform. The Apple I-phone is a perfect example. In 2007, Steve Jobs introduced the first Apple I-phone. No Doubt, it revolutionized telephone usage, but today, we are on generation 7 of the I-phone and soon to launch generation 8 on only the 10th anniversary of the original. However, many of the changes in the newer models along the way have not been that substantial or revolutionary. Regardless, consumers have been flocking to the Apple I- phone stores to purchase the new model year after year as soon as it is launched. The automobile and clothing manufacturers, as well as cell phone companies are just a few examples of how perceived obsolescence influences our modern consumerist society and fuels consumption in our current world economy.

And conspicuous consumption is the biggest contributor to global environmental destruction. The human person is not the problem; rather, the human person viewed as pure consumer is the problem. When we are viewed by society as having our socio-economic worth be defined in terms of what we buy and how much we consume, then ultimately both the environment and the common good will suffer. People who cannot restrain their consumption become the problem; primarily because the society and the modern Capitalist economy encourage and foster this behavior. A Distributist economy would discourage all forms of conspicuous consumption simply for consumption's sake.

Here are some of the words Pope Francis used in his latest Encyclical on the environment, "Praise Be," *Laudato Si,* as he relates consumerism to a lack of distributive justice:

> Climate change is a global problem with grave implications: environmental, social, economic, political and for the distribution of goods (LS #25)."

And:

> To blame population growth instead of extreme and selective consumerism by some, is one way of refusing to face the issues. It is an attempt to legitimize the present model of distribution, where a minority believes that it has the right to consume in a way which can never be universalized (LS #50).

Because Distributism's grounding is in the biblical and social tradition of the Catholic Church, there is an inherent responsibility for the natural order. The environment therefore, is not seen as a "thing" to be exploited, but as an extension of all life on the planet. Because of its rejection of a society built on consumption and its concern for the poorest in society there is both an economic and ethical foundation to support environmental protection. Therefore, in Distributism, all forms of pollution or any conspicuous consumption cannot be considered a "property right."

From Thomas Aquinas to Pope Francis, the church has maintained that private property always has a social mortgage. Like the church, because Distributism holds high regard for both the environment and a preferential option for the poor, the social mortgage on private property is held by those deprived of their distributive justice.

Private property and the common good are two key facets of Distributism economic theory. Under this system, most people would be able to earn a living without having to rely on the use of the property of others or their capital to do so. The "cooperative" approach advances beyond this perspective to recognize that such property and equipment may be "co-owned" by local communities larger than a family, e.g., extended families, partners in a business, agricultural or industrial co-ops. In Distributism, the growth of large numbers of small businesses, particularly those which are family owned, is nurtured and fostered. The theory also allows for the participation of larger corporations, but in most every case the corporation would have mainly employee-owners. Small business would also not be subject to unjust or unfavorable laws which have primarily served big business in the past and created monopolies as a result.

Ownership of private property would be a reality in a Distributist economy, whereas in a modern Capitalist economy it is no more than a fallacy. In this regard, Capitalism should really be called "Captivism," as credit holds us as captives. Our consumerist society has been built on the expansion of credit. Car loans, school loans, home loans, bank loans, business loans, huge credit card debt etc., initiated because of the ongoing process of conspicuous consumption, all have created the appearance of ownership. However, this is far from the reality, as they have mostly created debt for the worker which is owed to the few real capitalists who own the capital and who profit, often usuriously, from the system. The worker, who is really the consumer, becomes a debtor to keep the system in perpetual motion. He or she thinks themselves an owner, but they never usually are until they've paid three or four or sometimes ten times over.

And, some people never own what they have purchased with a credit card. If someone carries an average daily balance of $3,000 in credit card debt, their minimum payment would be around $60 a month. If the credit card charges a 15% APR, which is the national average today, interest alone would cost them approximately $425 per year to carry $3000 in purchased goods. In this system, some people will never get out of debt.

So, to move from a Capitalist society based on consumerism to a Distributist society based on solidarity will require a move away from a society of debtors and toward a society of owners. It will require families coming together in community and beginning to live a more frugal (or might I dare to say even sometimes a simple or an ascetic lifestyle). This will empower us to begin to use our God-given free will to reject the many desires and fanciful whims created by a society built on consumption and consumerism. It will diminish our dependence on "things" to satisfy our wants and allow us to recognize that God has already given us all we need. Finally, it will also begin to create the broader base of "capitalists" and owners, necessary for a Distributist society to function properly.

Distributism relies heavily on the Catholic Principles of Solidarity and Subsidiarity. Solidarity is about valuing the basic human dignity and rights of those in community and learning to respect who they are as individuals within families. It is a spirit of unity, whereby we are bonded with one another; including and especially the poorest, weakest, and most vulnerable in society. Solidarity is the glue that bonds us. Once again, subsidiarity holds that no larger unit (whether social, economic, or political) should perform a function which can be performed by a smaller unit (even as small as the family unit). The characteristic implication of subsidiarity and solidarity is participation, whereby persons either as individuals or in association with others, contribute to the cultural, economic, political and social life of the community. Participation plays a key role in Distributism and is a duty to be fulfilled by all, with a view to the common good.

Furthermore, regarding the relationship to government, Distributism maintains that it should be as small as possible and only as big as necessary.

St Thomas Aquinas has said in his *Summa*: "The will of God is the universal cause of all goods and . . . All power rests in God *(Summa*, T. Aquinas, Q.19, Art IV; Q.25, Art III)."[10]

In a Distributist society, government would understand that its first role is to recognize that all authoritative power comes from God. Government's role is then to participate in God's sovereignty. It should act on God's behalf to promote human dignity, protect human rights, pursue justice, and defend the interests of the poorest in society. In a society founded on the principles of distributive justice, it would require that the allocation of wealth, power, and resources be always evaluated as to its effects on persons whose basic material needs are going unmet. Government is also necessarily involved in protecting the entire economic order by implementing laws consistent with it for the benefit of the common good. In describing how the Principle of Subsidiarity works in government's role and the different levels of government, Pope John Paul II has said in his modern Social Letter, *On the One Hundredth Year,* echoing Pius XI:

> A community of a higher order should not interfere in the internal life of a community of a lower order, depriving the latter of its functions, but rather should support it in case of need and help to coordinate its activity with the

activities of the rest of society, always with a view of the common good (CA #48; QA # 184-186).

Some will say, "Distributism will never work given the size and scope of the economic system today." Our generation has certainly witnessed the globalization of economics. So, those naysayers would be partly right. Distributism cannot simply just replace Capitalism on any given day. It must begin as a movement first, a revolutionary groundswell because people want it, and see that the modern Capitalist system is just not working for most of the people in it. On the other hand, Distributism cannot function completely as a system within a system. It can only start that way. We are not speaking of anarchy here, but if you believe that putting people before things is a good starting point, then you are already a Distributist at heart.

The groundswell will also probably have to begin in the homes of Catholic families in solidarity because of its foundation having been laid on the ethical and socio-economic principle of distributive justice as formulated by the Social Teachings of the Catholic Church. This shouldn't imply that only Catholics would ultimately be living and working in this type of system, just that it would have to start somewhere and starting and flourishing in the family homes of the Catholic community would appear to be the best initial option. In the words of T.S. Eliot: "Home is where one starts from . . . in my end is my beginning."[11]

Those who say that Distributism cannot work because of the globalization of economics today also fail to recognize that Real Capitalism has evolved to attempt to operate within a global economic environment. It didn't begin that way. It is extremely narrow-minded to simply dismiss something only because it has been untried and untested. Chesterton maintained that people who thought this way had "locked themselves in the clean, well-lit prison of one idea."[12]

We have become a global society of conspicuous consumers under Capitalism. Unlike Capitalism, Distributism is not just an economic theory; it can become a manifestation of the existence of distributive justice present in society. Furthermore, it is a moot point to even try to establish that it cannot function in a system based on the globalization of economics. It is more a matter that globalization itself will eventually cease to function without a return to the localization and decentralization of society, economics, and politics. Distributism only appears complicated because economics in today's world has become so very complicated. But, it eventually could make economics, politics, and society simple again.

As with all paradox in Chesterton's writing, he will consistently point to a truth that is the opposite or in stark contradiction to what we expect. In *What I Saw in America*, Ch. 21, he writes:

> "Travel narrows the mind . . . The real purpose of travelling is to return . . . The true destination of every journey is home."[13]

"Home is where the heart is." This is the crux of the idea behind the economic theory of Distributism. Distributive justice, as a gift from God, is its foundation. Putting people before things can start the building process because Distributism can only be built by people who truly love God and their neighbor. They will then seek after justice and come together in solidarity with a willingness to equitably share their wealth, power and resources for the common good. Ultimately, Distributism as a potential economic system can only be brought to birth and nurtured by this nucleus of people as an extended family. On the other hand, it will never come to birth if we simply and naively expect that we will somehow bypass the many pangs of intensive labor involved first.

The exorcism of the Gerasene demoniac which appears in in Matthew, Mark, and Luke's Gospels is one of the 37 miracles performed by Jesus in the New Testament.[14] The story shows Jesus exorcising demons out of a man and sending them into a herd of swine, causing all the pigs to run headlong down a hill and drowning themselves in a lake. What makes this story so interesting is the upshot of the whole event. Following the miracle, the local townspeople end up asking Jesus to "get out of town." Why? Could it be because they believe he is going to ruin the whole economy there by doing things like this? But, there is a false safety in simply making "a preferential option for the status quo." The people seem to fear the removal of the pigs as their current income source more than they fear the many demons. They also seem to value the existing economy and their possessions more than they value the poor possessed man. Ultimately, they had a faulty value system which clouded their judgement as to what should have been their proper response to Jesus.

To move toward a society which is based on a Distributist economic model, will not be an easy undertaking and it will involve considerable change, sacrifice, receptivity, flexibility, and transformation to get rid of the many demons in our current society and economy. In the end, it would certainly be another miracle.

In conclusion: if we do somehow laboriously and miraculously bring to birth a Distributist economic system, it would not only have to begin with Catholics, but probably would have to be born in America as well; the current home of World Capitalism. This would then allow us as Americans to say that we expect to live out as a reality what we currently espouse in reciting the *Pledge of Allegiance*; that we are really becoming:

> "One nation, under God, indivisible, with liberty and justice for all."[15]

Notes

1. BEGINNINGS AND HISTORY

1. Pope Leo VIII, On the New Things, *Rerum Novarum,* Vatican Archives, 1891 http://w2.vatican.va/content/leo-xiii/en/encyclicals/documents/hf_l-xiii_enc_15051891_rerum-novarum.html
2. The One Hundredth Year, *Centessimus Annus,* John Paul II, 1991, http://w2.vatican.va/content/john-paul-ii/en/encyclicals/documents/hf_jp-ii_enc_01051991_centesimus-annus.html #11
3. Ibid see endnote 1
4. Ibid see endnote 1, Section #33
5. http://www.vatican.va/archive/hist_councils/ii_vatican_council/documents/vat-ii_decl_19651207_dignitatis-humanae_en.html and http://www.vatican.va/archive/hist_councils/ii_vatican_council/documents/vat-ii_cons_19651207_gaudium-et-spes_en.html
6. Ibid see endnote #1
7. New American Bible, St. Joseph and Revised Edition, US Conference of Catholic Bishops, United States Catholic Conference, (New York, N.Y.: Catholic Book Publishing Company, 1970) see also http://www.usccb.org/bible/books-of-the-bible/index.cfm
8. Ibid see endnote #7
9. Ibid see endnote #7
10. Ibid see endnote #7
11. Ibid see endnote #7
12. Ibid see endnote #7

2. HUMAN DIGNITY; LOVE OF GOD AND NEIGHBOR

1. Ibid see endnote #7
2. Thomas Aquinas, Summa Theologica, from The New Advent Website, Kevin Knight, (Denver, Colorado: Advent International, 2017) http://www.newadvent.org/summa/4004.htm#article5
3. Ibid see footnote #7

4. "neighbor." Douglas Harper, ed., Online Etymology Dictionary found at http://www.etymonline.com/index.php?allowed_in_frame=0&search=neighbor
5. Ibid see endnote #7
6. Ibid see endnote #7

3. FAMILY AND COMMUNITY; SOCIAL AND ECONOMIC JUSTICE

1. Vatican Archives, Dogmatic Constitution on the Church, *Lumen Gentium* #11, Vatican II, http://www.vatican.va/archive/hist_councils/ii_vatican_council/documents/vat-ii_const_19641121_lumen-gentium_en.html
2. Facts About Income Inequality, Pew Research Center Study, 2014, http://www.pewresearch.org/fact-tank/2014/01/07/5-facts-about-economic-inequality/
3. Catechism of the Catholic Church, CC 2424-2429, Part III, Sec. 2, Ch. 2, Vatican Archives, http://www.vatican.va/archive/ccc_css/archive/catechism/p3s2c2a7.htm
4. Ibid See endnote #7

4. RIGHTS AND DUTIES; SOCIALIZATION, SOLIDARITY AND SUBSIDIARITY

1. "Justice" Etymology Dictionary, see Endnote #16, http://www.etymonline.com/index.php?allowed_in_frame=0&search=justice
2. Vatican Archives, John Paul II, *Centessimus Annus* # 47 human rights, 1991, http://w2.vatican.va/content/john-paul-ii/en/encyclicals/documents/hf_jp-ii_enc_01051991_centesimus-annus.html
3. Lincoln, Abraham, *Collected Works on Government,* Vol II, Fragment on Government, P. 221, 1854 https://quod.lib.umich.edu/l/lincoln/lincoln2/1:261?rgn=div1;view=fulltext

5. THE ROLE OF GOVERNMENT; PREFERENTIAL OPTION FOR THE POOR

1. Vatican Archives, Pastoral Constitution on the Church, *Gaudium et Spes* #63, Vatican II, 1965 http://www.vatican.va/archive/hist_councils/ii_vatican_council/documents/vat-ii_cons_19651207_gaudium-et-spes_en.html
2. Pedro Arrupe, S.J., Letter, 1968 http://www.uscatholic.org/articles/201501/what-preferential-option-poor-29649
3. See above http://www.uscatholic.org/articles/201501/what-preferential-option-poor-29649
4. Vatican Archives, John Paul II, *Centessimus Annus,* Benedict XVI, *Caritas in Veritate,* Francis, *Evangelli Gaudium*
5. Ibid see endnote # 7 NAB
6. Ibid see endnote # 21, CC 1397 http://www.vatican.va/archive/ccc_css/archive/catechism/p3s2c2a7.htm
7. Vatican Archives, Pastoral Constitution on the Church, *Gaudium et Spes*, # 1, VAT II, 1965
8. St. Lawrence, Rev. Don Miller, O.F.M., *Fransiscan Media,* 2016

6. PARTICIPATION AND WORK; FREEDOM AND LIFE

1. Ibid, see endnote #1
2. Vatican Archives, Declaration on Religious Freedom, *Dignitatis Humanae,* VAT II, 1965 http://www.vatican.va/archive/hist_councils/ii_vatican_council/documents/vat-ii_decl_19651207_dignitatis-humanae_en.html
3. Vatican Archives, The Gospel of Life, *Evangelium Vitae,* John Paul II, 1995 http://w2.vatican.va/content/john-paul-ii/en/encyclicals/documents/hf_jp-ii_enc_25031995_evangelium-vitae.html

7. THE MARKETPLACE AND CONSUMERISM; RESPECT FOR GOD'S CREATION— THE ENVIRONMENT

1. Augustine, Confessions, Book I, see the New Advent Website at http://www.newadvent.org/fathers/110101.htm
2. Vatican Archives, Praise Be, Letter on the Environment, Laudato Si, #16, Francis, 2015 http://w2.vatican.va/content/francesco/en/encyclicals/documents/papa-francesco_20150524_enciclica-laudato-si.html
3. Ibid, "economy" see endnote #16 http://www.etymonline.com/index.php?allowed_in_frame=0&search=economy
4. Vatican Archives, The Joy of the Gospel, *Evangelii Gaudium*#56, Francis, 2014 http://w2.vatican.va/content/francesco/en/apost_exhortations/documents/papa-francesco_esortazione-ap_20131124_evangelii-gaudium.html

8. EVANGELIZATION-COME HOLY SPIRIT

1. Ibid NAB, see endnote # 7
2. Ibid Praise Be, *Laudato Si*, see endnote # 38
3. Ibid see endnote # 16, *"dynamis,"* http://www.etymonline.com/index.php?allowed_in_frame=0&search=dynamis
4. Ibid NAB, see endnote # 7
5. Come Holy Spirit, *Prayer to the Holy Spirit,* Catholic Online, 2017 http://www.catholic.org/prayers/prayer.php?p=1405
6. Vatican Archives, Mother and Teacher, *Mater et Magistra* # 236, John XXXIII, 1961 http://w2.vatican.va/content/john-xxiii/en/encyclicals/documents/hf_j-xxiii_enc_15051961_mater.html
7. Holy Spirit Hymn, *Veni Creator Spiritus,* Catholic Online, 2017 http://www.catholic.org/prayers/prayer.php?p=332
8. Ibid see endnote #1
9. Ibid see endnote # 38

9. ON THE NEW THINGS-(*RERUM NOVARUM*), POPE LEO XIII, 1891*

1. Ibid see endnote #1 http://w2.vatican.va/content/leo-xiii/en/encyclicals/documents/hf_l-xiii_enc_15051891_rerum-novarum.html
2. Ibid see endnote # 1
3. Ibid see endnote #1 (sec. 23)
4. G.K. Chesterton, *Three Works on Distributism*, (New York, N.Y.; McGraw Hill, 2009 https://www.amazon.com/Three-Works-Distributism-G-Chesterton/dp/1449511228
5. Preferential Option for the Poor, *Centessimus Annus*, # 11 John Paul II, 1991 http://w2.vatican.va/content/john-paul-ii/en/encyclicals/documents/hf_jp-ii_enc_01051991_centesimus-annus.html
6. Ibid see endnote #1 (RN# 24)
7. Ibid NAB see endnote # 7
8. Temporal and Eternal, Helm, Paul, "Eternity", *The Stanford Encyclopedia of Philosophy* (Spring 2014 Edition), Edward N. Zalta (ed.), URL = <https://plato.stanford.edu/archives/spr2014/entries/eternity see also Hickey, Michael, *Get To The End*, Eternity and the End of Time, p. 25 (Lanham, MD, University Press of America, 2016) https://www.amazon.com/Get-End-Catholics-View-Times/dp/0761867333
9. Pastoral Constitution on the Church, *Gaudium et Spes*, preface, Vatican II, 1965 http://www.vatican.va/archive/hist_councils/ii_vatican_council/documents/vat-ii_cons_19651207_gaudium-et-spes_en.html

10. ON THE FORTIETH YEAR-(*QUADRAGESIMO ANNO*), PIUS XI, 1931*

1. Ibid see endnote 60 # 79-80
2. Ibid see endnote 60 # 5, 57, 60, 61, 76, 36
3. Ibid see endnote 60 # 129, 136

11. SOCIAL LETTERS OF POPE JOHN XXIII

1. Vatican Archives, Mother and Teacher, *Mater et Magistra,* John XXIII, 1961 http://w2.vatican.va/content/john-xxiii/en/encyclicals/documents/hf_j-xxiii_enc_15051961_mater.html
2. Ibid see endnote #1
3. Ibid see endnote # 60
4. Ibid see endnote # 64, “solidarity,” sections MM #23, 146, 155-157, 190
5. Ibid see endnote #64, “solidarity,” sections # 117, 152
6. Ibid see endnote # 64, “Marxism,” section # 23
7. Marx, Karl, Critique of *Hegel's Philosophy of Right,* Die Religion das Opium des Volkes, 1843, Phrase Finder http://www.phrases.org.uk/meanings/300700.html
8. Ibid see endnote # 64, sections # 46, 117, 48
9. Ibid see endnote # 64, “distributive justice,” sections # 48, 74, 82-83, 113-115, 136, 168
10. Ibid see endnote # 64, sections 218-226
11. Vatican Archives, Peace on Earth, *Pacem in Terris,* John XXIII, 1963 http://w2.vatican.va/content/john-xxiii/en/encyclicals/documents/hf_j-xxiii_enc_11041963_pacem.html
12. Ibid see endnote # 74, “solidarity,” sections 140-141

13. Ibid see endnote # 74, "rights," sections 11-27
14. Ibid see endnote # 74, "duties," sections 28-34
15. Ibid see endnote # 74, "Truth, Justice, Love, Freedom, sections 35-36
16. Ibid see endnote # 59 and endnote # 35
17. Ibid see endnote # 74, "distributive justice," sections 35-56
18. John XXIII, New York Times, Opinion, "Calling for a World Community," (New York, N. Y.; A.M. Rosenthal, ed., April 11, 1963) http://www.nytimes.com/2002/12/25/opinion/peace-on-earth.html

12. SOCIAL LETTERS OF VATICAN COUNCIL II, 1965

1. Preface Vatican II Archives see http://www.vatican.va/archive/hist_councils/ii_vatican_council/documents/vat-ii_cons_19651207_gaudium-et-spes_en.html
2. Murray, John Courtney, We Hold These Truths, (Rowman &Littlefield/Sheed & Ward; Lanham Maryland, 1960)
3. Pope Pius IX, Syllabus of Errors Condemned, see Vatican Archives, Papal Encyclicals, http://www.papalencyclicals.net/Pius09/p9syll.htm
4. Vatican Archives; Dignitatis Humanae, see http://www.vatican.va/archive/hist_councils/ii_vatican_council/documents/vat-ii_decl_19651207_dignitatis-humanae_en.html
5. Vatican II Archives, Pastoral Constitution on the Church, see http://www.vatican.va/archive/hist_councils/ii_vatican_council/documents/vat-ii_cons_19651207_gaudium-et-spes_en.html
6. Vatican II Archives, Decree on the Apostolate of the Laity, see http://www.vatican.va/archive/hist_councils/ii_vatican_council/documents/vat-ii_decree_19651118_apostolicam-actuositatem_en.html
7. Ibid see endnote # 85

13. SOCIAL LETTERS OF POPE PAUL VI

1. Ibid see endnotes # 1, # 60, # 64, # 74
2. Vatican Archives, On the Development of Peoples, see http://w2.vatican.va/content/paul-vi/en/encyclicals/documents/hf_p-vi_enc_26031967_populorum.html
3. Ibid see endnote #1
4. Vatican Archives, On the Eightieth Year see http://w2.vatican.va/content/paul-vi/en/apost_letters/documents/hf_p-vi_apl_19710514_octogesima-adveniens.html

14. SOCIAL LETTERS OF JOHN PAUL II, 1981-1987

1. Ibid see endnote # 1
2. PBS, John Paul II and the Fall of Communism, (Barnes Jane; PBS, Frontline, 1979) see http://www.pbs.org/wgbh/pages/frontline/shows/pope/communism/
3. Vatican Archives, On Human Work, see https://w2.vatican.va/content/john-paul-ii/en/encyclicals/documents/hf_jp-ii_enc_14091981_laborem-exercens.html
4. Vatican Archives, The Progress of Peoples, see http://w2.vatican.va/content/paul-vi/en/encyclicals/documents/hf_p-vi_enc_26031967_populorum.html

5. (SS # 42) Vatican Archives, The Social Concern of the Church, see http://w2.vatican.va/content/john-paul-ii/en/encyclicals/documents/hf_jp-ii_enc_30121987_sollicitudo-rei-socialis.html
6. Ibid see endnote #7
7. Ibid see endnote # 96

15. SOCIAL LETTERS OF JOHN PAUL II, 1991-1995

1. Ibid see endnote # 1
2. Vatican Archives, On the 100 Years, see http://w2.vatican.va/content/john-paul-ii/en/encyclicals/documents/hf_jp-ii_enc_01051991_centesimus-annus.html
3. Ibid NAB see endnote # 7
4. Ibid NAB see endnote # 7
5. Vatican Archives, The Gospel of Life, see http://w2.vatican.va/content/john-paul-ii/en/encyclicals/documents/hf_jp-ii_enc_25031995_evangelium-vitae.html

16. SOCIAL LETTER OF POPE BENEDICT XVI, 2009

1. Ibid see endnote # 7
2. Vatican Archives, On the Progress of Peoples, see http://w2.vatican.va/content/paul-vi/en/encyclicals/documents/hf_p-vi_enc_26031967_populorum.html
3. Ibid NAB see endnote # 7
4. Vatican Archives, Charity in Truth, see http://w2.vatican.va/content/benedict-xvi/en/encyclicals/documents/hf_ben-xvi_enc_20090629_caritas-in-veritate.html

17. SOCIAL LETTERS OF POPE FRANCIS, 2013-2015

1. Aquinas, Thomas, Summa Theologica, Second Part of the Second Part, Mercy; Q. 30 see the new Advent Website at http://www.newadvent.org/summa/3030.htm
2. Ibid NAB see endnote # 7
3. Ibid NAB see endnote # 7
4. Vatican Archives, The Joy of the Gospel, see http://w2.vatican.va/content/francesco/en/apost_exhortations/documents/papa-francesco_esortazione-ap_20131124_evangelii-gaudium.html
5. Canticle of St Francis, see http://www.catholic.org/prayers/prayer.php?p=3188 Ibid, also see endnotes # 94, # 95, # 96, # 105, # 108
6. Vatican Archives, Praise Be, On Care for our Common Home, see http://w2.vatican.va/content/francesco/en/encyclicals/documents/papa-francesco_20150524_enciclica-laudato-si.html

18. ROOTS OF DISTRIBUTIVE JUSTICE

1. Ibid see endnote # 1
2. Ibid see endnote # 7

3. Ibid see endnote # 7
4. Ibid see endnote # 7
5. Ibid see endnote # 7
6. Aristotle, Nichomachean Ethics and Politics, see The Internet Classics Archives http://classics.mit.edu/Aristotle/nicomachaen.5.v.html and http://classics.mit.edu/Aristotle/politics.html
7. Ibid see endnote # 120, Book V, Justice
8. Maimonides, Moses; Guide for the Perplexed, (Sacred Texts; Friedlander, 1904) see Sacred Texts http://www.sacred-texts.com/jud/gfp/gfp006.htm
9. Maimonides, Moses; Laws on Gifts for the Poor, Treatises on Justice, (Williamsburg, Virginia; College of William and Mary, Dept. of Religion Books, Dr. Marc Raphael, ed., 2003) see https://www.amazon.com/Gifts-Poor-Maimonides-Treatise-Tzedakah/dp/1519515464
10. Ibid see endnote # 122
11. Aquinas, Thomas; Summa Theologica, see new Advent Website at http://www.newadvent.org/summa/
12. Ibid see endnote # 125
13. Ibid see endnote # 1
14. Ibid see endnote # 125, also see Vatican Archives; Catechism of the Catholic Church, see http://www.vatican.va/archive/ENG0015/_INDEX.HTM

19. DISTRIBUTIVE JUSTICE IN THE MODERN PAPAL SOCIAL LETTERS- THE FOUNDATIONAL LETTERS

1. Ibid see endnote # 1
2. Chesterton, Gilbert K.; Outline of Sanity (Norfolk, Va.; I.H.S. Press, 1927); Belloc, Hilaire, The Servile State (London, Eng., Neill & Co., T. N. Foules, ed., 1912)
3. Ibid see endnote # 60
4. Ibid see endnote 60 # 5, 57, 60, 61, 76, 36
5. Ibid see endnote # 64
6. Ibid see endnote # 74

20. DISTRIBUTIVE JUSTICE IN THE SOCIAL LETTERS OF POPE JOHN XXIII; AND VATICAN COUNCIL II

1. Ibid see endnote # 64
2. Ibid see endnote # 1
3. Ibid see endnote # 60, QA # 35
4. Ibid see endnote # 64, "distributive justice," sections # 48, 74, 82-83, 113-115, 136, 168
5. Ibid see endnote # 74
6. Ibid see endnote # 74 sec. 92; also see Augustine, De Civitate Dei, lib. IV, c. 4; PL 41. 115; cf. Pius XII's broadcast message, Christmas 1939, AAS 32 (1940) 5-13
7. Vatican Archives, Vatican II, Document on Religious Freedom, see http://www.vatican.va/archive/hist_councils/ii_vatican_council/documents/vat-ii_decl_19651207_dignitatis-humanae_en.html
8. Vatican archives, Vatican II, Pastoral Constitution on the Church, see http://www.vatican.va/archive/hist_councils/ii_vatican_council/documents/vat-ii_cons_19651207_gaudium-et-spes_en.html

9. Ibid see endnote # 141, fn. # 10

21. DISTRIBUTIVE JUSTICE IN THE SOCIAL LETTERS OF POPE PAUL VI

1. Ibid see endnote # 105
2. Ibid see endnote # 1
3. Ibid see endnote # 1
4. Vatican Archives, Eightieth Year, see http://w2.vatican.va/content/paul-vi/en/apost_letters/documents/hf_p-vi_apl_19710514_octogesima-adveniens.html

22. DISTRIBUTIVE JUSTICE IN THE SOCIAL LETTERS OF POPE JOHN PAUL II, 1981-1991

1. Vatican Archives, Through Work, see https://w2.vatican.va/content/john-paul-ii/en/encyclicals/documents/hf_jp-ii_enc_14091981_laborem-exercens.html
2. Ibid see endnote # 1
3. Ibid see endnote # 60
4. Vatican Archives, The Social Concern of the Church, see http://w2.vatican.va/content/john-paul-ii/en/encyclicals/documents/hf_jp-ii_enc_30121987_sollicitudo-rei-socialis.html
5. Vatican Archives, The One Hundredth Year, see http://w2.vatican.va/content/john-paul-ii/en/encyclicals/documents/hf_jp-ii_enc_01051991_centesimus-annus.html
6. Ibid see endnote # 1

23. DISTRIBUTIVE JUSTICE IN THE SOCIAL LETTERS OF POPE JOHN PAUL II, 1995 AND POPE BENEDICT XVI, 2009

1. Vatican Archives, The Gospel of Life, see http://w2.vatican.va/content/john-paul-ii/en/encyclicals/documents/hf_jp-ii_enc_25031995_evangelium-vitae.html
2. Vatican Archives, Charity in Truth, see http://w2.vatican.va/content/benedict-xvi/en/encyclicals/documents/hf_ben-xvi_enc_20090629_caritas-in-veritate.html
3. Ibid see endnote # 1

24. DISTRIBUTIVE JUSTICE IN THE SOCIAL LETTERS OF POPE FRANCIS

1. Vatican Archives, The Joy of the Gospel, see http://w2.vatican.va/content/francesco/en/apost_exhortations/documents/papa-francesco_esortazione-ap_20131124_evangelii-gaudium.html
2. Ibid NAB see endnote # 7

3. Vatican Archives, Praise Be, On Care for our Common Home, see http://w2.vatican.va/content/francesco/en/encyclicals/documents/papa-francesco_20150524_enciclica-laudato-si.html
4. Ibid see endnote # 156, f. 73; see also Vatican Archives, John Paul II, Social Letter, On the Social Concern of the Church, Sollicitudo Rei Socialis (30 December 1987), 33: AAS 80 (1988), 557

25. FROM DISTRIBUTIVE JUSTICE TO DISTRIBUTISM

1. Ibid see endnote #1
2. G.K. Chesterton and Hilaire Belloc; Distributism, Project Gutenberg; World Heritage Encyclopedia, see http://www.gutenberg.us/articles/eng/Distributism
3. Aquinas, Thomas; Summa I & II, Q. # 106; Aroney, Nicholas; Subsidiarity in the Writings of Aristotle and Aquinas, Ch. 2, see file:///C:/Users/mike/Downloads/9789401788090-c2%20(2).pdf
4. Chesterton, G.K.; Collected Works of G.K. Chesterton, Volume IV, The Superstition of Divorce, Ch. 3, (San Francisco, CA; Ignatius Press, 1987)
5. Ibid #16, Etymonline.com; "economics," see http://www.etymonline.com/index.php?allowed_in_frame=0&search=economics
6. Chesterton, G.K., Nolan James; What They Saw in America, p. 147 (NY, NY; Cambridge University Press, 2016)
7. Chesterton, G.K.; Orthodoxy, p.11 (London, England; John Lane Pub., 1909)
8. Chesterton, G.K.; Illustrated London News, January 3, 1914, Volume XXX, no. 17, see also https://books.google.com/books?id=ZmA4AQAAMAAJ&pg=PA4&lpg=PA4&dq=Chesterton%E2%80%99s:+%E2%80%9CThere+is+nothing+queerer+today+than+the+importance+of+unimportant+things;+except,+of+course,+the+unimportance+of+important&source=bl&ots=QMMmpISBHt&sig=IAF_GacWUQ6gawZpF24tv9h7AUo&hl=en&sa=X&ved=0ahUKEwiKw_iVzcDVAhVFVyYKHcMACiwQ6AEIOzAD#v=onepage&q=Chesterton%E2%80%99s%3A%20%E2%80%9CThere%20is%20nothing%20queerer%20today%20than%20the%20importance%20of%20unimportant%20things%3B%20except%2C%20of%20course%2C%20the%20unimportance%20of%20important&f=false
9. Chesterton, G.K.; Outline of Sanity, p.7, (NY, NY; Dodd Mead & Co., 1927)
10. Ibid see endnote #1 and endnote #60

26. DISTRIBUTISM-TOWARD A NEW ECONOMY

1. See the Vatican Archives, Website Catholic Social Teaching/Encyclicals http://www.catholicsocialteaching.org.uk/principles/documents/
2. Ibid see #171
3. Ibid # 1, Sec. #33
4. Chesterton, G.K.; Outline of Sanity, (London, England; Read Books Ltd., 2013) see also https://www.amazon.com/Outline-Sanity-G-K-Chesterton/dp/1447418085/ref=pd_lpo_sbs_14_t_0?_encoding=UTF8&psc=1&refRID=786PAGMAY81B6X6XZ39R
5. Oxfam America Report, January, 2017, see https://www.oxfam.org/en/pressroom/pressreleases/2017-01-16/just-8-men-own-same-wealth-half-world
6. Stone, Oliver; Douglas, Michael, movie Wall Street, Money Never Sleeps, 1987, see https://www.youtube.com/watch?v=PF_iorX_MAw
7. Ibid see # 171
8. Ibid see #1, Sec. 11-14, see also New Advent Website/Aquinas, Thomas, Summa; IIa-IIae, q. lxvi, art. 2, Answer.

9. Veblen, Thorstein; Theory of the Leisure Class/An Economic Study of Institutions, (NY, NY; Macmillan & Co, 1899)

10. Ibid # 125, see New Advent Website, *(Summa*, T. Aquinas, Q.19, Art IV; Q.25, Art III), http://www.newadvent.org/summa/

11. Eliot, T.S.;The Four Quartets/East Coker #5

12. Chesterton, G. K.; Orthodoxy/ The Maniac, p. 5 (London, England; Read Books Ltd., 2013) see also http://www.pagebypagebooks.com/Gilbert_K_Chesterton/Orthodoxy/The_Maniac_p5.html

13. Chesterton, G. K.; What I Saw in America, ch. 21 (London, England; Aeterna Press, 1968)

14. Ibid NAB, see # 7

15. Bellamy, Francis; Pledge of Allegiance, 1892, Revised 1923 & 1954, see http://www.ushistory.org/documents/pledge.htm

Index